The Complete Country Business Guide

Lisa Rogak

Williams Hill Publishing
Grafton, New Hampshire

This publication is designed to provide accurate and authoritative information in regard to the subject matter covered. It is sold with the understanding that the publisher is not engaged in rendering legal, accounting, or other professional services. If legal advice or other expert assistance is required, the services of a competent professional person should be sought.

First Edition

Printed in the United States of America

10 9 8 7 6 5 4 3 2 1

Publisher's Cataloging-in-Publication
Shaw, Lisa Angowski Rogak.
    The complete country business guide : everything you need to
know to become a rural entrepreneur / Lisa Rogak. — 1st ed.
        p. cm.
    Includes index.
    Preassigned LCCN: 98-96672
    ISBN: 0-9652502-1-0
    1. Rural industries—Management. 2. Small business—
Management. 3. Entrepreneurship.   I. Title.

HD2330.S43 1998   658.02'2'091734
                         QBI98-1360

Published by Williams Hill Publishing
RR 1 Box 1234
Kinsman Highway
Grafton NH 03240
603-523-7877
info@movetothecountry.com

www.ramtac-whc.com
www.movetothecountry.com
www.litterature.com

BK
$24.95

For Gregg,

the first of many

Contents

Contents

Contents

Introduction

So You Want to Run A Country Business...

It seems that two of the most popular trends of the 90s and early 21st century—moving to the country, and running your own business—have combined to create the one kind of lifestyle that, to many people, represents the most perfect kind of life possible.

Of course any kind of life that seems like the one solution that will make everything in your life fall into place does have its downsides: frequent power outages on the one hand, not knowing when to stop working on the other, especially if you work from home.

However, since I've been running a country business of my own since 1988, with no plans to change ever, I can tell you that the pleasures of running your own show in an uncrowded small town far outweigh the downsides. After all, the challenges of living a sometimes isolated rural life mean that you'll merely need to find a way to meet these disadvantages head-on. After the monumental ice storm of January 1998 hit my mountain with a vengeance, leaving me without power, heat or water for more than a week, I merely transferred my base of operations to a friend's house. I also learned to use the occasion as a well-deserved excuse to take a break. That's why it never ceases to amuse me whenever I turn on the radio and hear that people in some distant overcrowded smoggy metropolitan area have been without power for 23 minutes or without water for an entire day. Even though running your own business means you're in control, whenever an outside influence beyond your control forces you to give it up, at least temporarily, throw up your hands and take a break. What else can you do? This is one of the hidden joys not only of running a country-based business but of living in the country overall.

With this in mind, if you're reading this guide, you probably fall into one of three categories:

1) You live in the city or suburbs and want to move to the country and run your own business to provide your livelihood;
2) You already live in the country and want specific information on how to start a business that takes your own needs into consideration; or
3) You already live in the country and run a business, but want some detailed information on how you can make it even more profitable than it already is.

I've designed *The Complete Country Business Guide* as a training manual of sorts. That's why there's lots of space in the margins on each page to scribble in, take notes, write down your hopes and dreams and ideas for some crazy business that might just happen to fly.

And because this is a training manual, I'm constantly looking to improve it and include new information, ideas, and great country businesses in future editions of *The Complete Country Business Guide*. So if you have any specific questions on any issue about starting or running a country business, let me know. Get in touch by email, fax, snail mail, whatever. I'll address your question and include this new information in the next edition.

Sincerely,

Lisa Rogak

Chapter One

What It's Like to Run
A Country Business

Though millions of people dream about running their own businesses in the country—and many do this in order to become as self-sufficient in their lives as possible—for many the stress of moving to a different area and culture is difficult enough without the stress of starting a new business. With that said, let me spell out the advantages of running a business in the country as opposed to working at a job.

Four Good Reasons
To Start a Rural Business

Here are four reasons why you should plan to start a business in the country and not find a job. But since I run my own rural business, you should keep in mind that I'm biased.

1) You can move to the country now, not later.

2) Most rural jobs that you'll be able to find right away tend to pay less than a living wage.

3) Finding a job that's comparable to the well-paying job you have now is difficult, and in popular areas you'll find yourself up against a lot of competition. A friend who moved from New York City to Missoula, Montana, a few years ago applied for a part-time job with the university that paid $12 an hour, which is phenomenally high for the area. She got the job, but had to compete against more than 100 equally qualified people.

4) You can start or plan your business *before* you move if it's not strictly a local business. In some areas, you're going to be viewed with derision if you move to the country and decide you're going to make your living solely from selling jam and homemade pastries to the general store. I feel you should either give a project like this some time before you start (The local reaction could be "Who does she think she is? She just moved in last week from Boston!") or else focus on the retail and service opportunities in a tourist area, where most people come from somewhere else and don't care where you came from.

The Dream Country Business

Because it's such a common rural fantasy for many city dwellers, here's the story of how one couple moved from New York City to Vermont to start a country inn. But first, read the following ad:

Help Wanted: Couple to cook, clean, and serve as surrogate family to thousands of strangers who stay in your home each year. Must always smile, work 18-hour days, be skilled in home repair and yard work, and able to perform monetary miracles in order to pay bills when bank account is dangerously low. Business comes first; any crumbs left over are yours.

Salary: Petty cash plus room and board.

Would you answer this hypothetical ad?

Probably not, even though you're probably one of countless people who dream of buying a country inn.

Max and Merrily Comins own and operate the Kedron Valley Inn in South Woodstock, Vermont, a 28-room inn with a 100-seat restaurant. In their previous life in New York, Max worked on Wall Street and Merrily worked in research and marketing for a database company. They had long fantasized about owning a country inn, and finally made the move in 1985.

They visited 70 different inns before deciding on the Kedron. "I wanted to make it into the kind of place I would want to visit," says Max. In its twelve years of operation, the inn is just the way he wants it, but it hasn't been easy. "The first three years we literally worked all the time," says Merrily. They opted for a large inn instead of a smaller one with 8 to 10 rooms, because with those "you spend a lot of your time chopping vegetables and cleaning guest rooms."

You might think that you wouldn't mind that if you could live in the country. "But," says Merrily, "try five years of chopping vegetables and cleaning potties if you have a college degree and have lived in a metropolitan area." With a large inn, the Comins can hire more support staff and can choose to do the things that they find more interesting with their business backgrounds.

"We're constantly hosting people who think that running away to run a country inn is the dream of a lifetime, and isn't it wonderful we're here in the great outdoors," says Merrily. "In the first four years we were here, we went skiing once, and we're just ten minutes from Killington. We had planned to go three other times, but each time we went out the door, something happened and we had to stay."

When it's quiet, Max says that he works up to 80 hours a week. During foliage season, he works more than 100 hours, and that's with a maximum staff of 40. Their 14-year-old son Drew helps out, and Merrily says that innkeeping has its advantages when raising a child, but it can get sticky at times. Once when Drew was younger, she had to do the payroll one week when Drew was sick and Max was away. "So I did it on my kitchen floor with a Mickey Mouse calculator and with Drew throwing up into a stewpot," she says.

The inn does 50 percent of its business in August, September, and October. It was only after they bought the inn that Max and Merrily discovered that their business styles were radically different. "I'm more analytical, Max is more shoot-from-the-hip," says Merrily. "And I miss some things about the city. One reason Max is happier with his lifestyle is because he hated New York. I didn't."

Max admits that the inn is his social life. "I'm over at the inn every night we serve dinner so I can see virtually every guest who comes," he says. "I feel guilty when I don't. Most of the people who come here are here for that reason alone. That's what makes one inn different from another, and I think it's why we have so much repeat business. I strive to make everyone feel like they have come to my home, and not a hotel or a restaurant."

He adds that guests think it's easy to walk around and greet everyone—which he agrees with—but he adds that it's also very tiring and time-consuming.

If you're not scared off, Merrily has some advice. "Get a professional to help you in your search to define your needs and to structure financing. I would also serve as an assistant innkeeper at somebody else's inn in Vermont during foliage season for three months. At the end of that time, you'll have a good idea of what innkeeping is like."

Quick-Start Country Businesses

A common feature of country living which always surprises the newcomer is the number of people who make a living at several enterprises, says Barbara Radcliffe Rogers.

In the city, people tend to have a career, a profession, a job. Maybe they moonlight a little, but they have one basic line of work. Not so in the country. A farmer may drive the school bus, rent canoes, run a campground in the back forty, and/or repair small engines. The local librarian may do tailoring and sell quilts at craft shows. None of these provides enough income alone, but together they suffice.

Some of the enterprises are seasonal—tapping trees for maple, guiding hunters, selling pumpkins or making Christmas wreaths. Others are year-round, or can be done between seasons. These smaller businesses are particularly attractive to newcomers who are still looking around for a permanent line of work.

Whether they are an income supplement to help defray renovations on a house or an interim measure until you are settled, you should plan an enterprise carefully since, surprisingly often, one that began as a moonlighting or stopgap measure turns into a permanent, full-time business.

A few general considerations come first, before you decide what kind of small business to begin. Ask yourself the following questions:

♦ What do I know best? Frequently, skills that you've acquired through hobbies, previous jobs or personal interests can be expanded into businesses.

♦ How much startup investment will it take? Concentrate on those with the least capital outlay, especially if you plan this to be a temporary or part-time activity.

♦ Can I do it in or from my own home? A business that requires renting extra space may require too much investment for temporary or part-time work.

♦ Is this something I could enjoy doing full-time? If not, it might not be a wise choice for part-time, either.

♦ Does this business fit the area I live in? Tarot readings might be very popular in a city that serves as the home to a large alternative and holistic community like Brattleboro, Vermont, but less so in the isolated farm country of East Corinth, Vermont.

♦ Is someone already doing it, and if so, is there ample business for two? There is no faster way to alienate new neighbors than entering into direct competition with the livelihood of a local resident.

Three popular areas for small businesses in rural areas are food, farm and garden, and services. Here are some ideas for each:

Types of Food Businesses

Home-baked goods, gourmet preserves, wild fruit jams and jellies, decorated cakes, herb and spice blends, catering parties or weddings, fudge or candy making.

Tips for Food Businesses

♦ Try something unusual. Instead of jams, make salad dressings.

♦ Your recipes don't have to be really unique, as long as your ingredients are good and you make a tasty product.

♦ If you plan to sell your product to local residents instead of tourists or summer people, avoid products that reek of snob appeal or that are too much associated with country life. Either one can annoy neighbors, who may find a snob appeal product patronizing ("I can't believe I couldn't find decent croissants here!") or resent your assumption that just because you've moved to the country you can make better pies than Mrs. Green.

♦ Unless your local general store caters to tourists as well as locals, don't expect them to stock your product. Look for shops in larger towns or tourist areas, especially if your product falls in the "gourmet" line.

♦ Always donate some of your product to local bake sales and charity events. This will build your reputation in your own town without you appearing pushy or as though you were trying to take advantage of new friendships.

Types of Farm & Garden Businesses

Growing and selling pumpkins, dried flowers for the florist trade, wreaths made from dried flowers you have grown or collected in the wild, cone and seed wreaths, Christmas trees (which you can either grow or buy wholesale) balsam Christmas wreaths (which you make or buy wholesale), fresh herbs for the restaurant trade.

Tips for Farm & Garden Businesses

♦ Don't begin a farm business that involves growing crops unless you know how. Gardens are notoriously undependable sources of income, especially for beginners.

♦ Ask around to see who already sells pumpkins, Christmas trees, etc. Don't expect to survive entirely on local business—join a farmer's market, arrange to sell in a nearby population center, or make contacts at grocery stores and specialty shops in the area.

♦ Make sure you have a market lined up before you begin—a florist shop in a nearby city may buy your wreaths or dried flowers, or a church bazaar may buy them to sell or let you sell there for a commission.

Types of Service Businesses

Dressmaking and tailoring, small appliance repair, child care, house sitting (in wealthier towns), landscaping and yard work, housework, thrift shop, pet care (in wealthy communities), income tax preparation, parties, magic shows, sport or other lessons.

Tips for Service Businesses

♦ Some of these businesses, such as child care, may require licensing—be sure to check with your state.

♦ Be careful of businesses where you have to wait for your neighbors to come to you. It's best to have a contact that can use your services, such as a clothing store that will send you their alterations.

♦ If you live in a touristy area, find ways to advertise to tourists, especially if your service is in the entertainment or sports field.

♦ To advertise and make money at the same time, teach classes, either on your own or sponsored by the local library or school. Give programs to local clubs free of charge, showing how to do some facet of your work.

Rural Government & Your Country Business

One of the great fallacies of moving to the country is that you will be leaving behind government interference into your life. It is true that rules are often far more relaxed in rural areas—few towns have ordinances that govern the color of our house, for example, as some city neighborhoods do—and rural areas generally give a lot more leeway to the homeowner who prefers to do his or her own construction and repairs. But small towns do take an interest in businesses within their bounds. Just how much of an interest and how friendly, is what you need to discover before you buy the property or open your shop.

While most of your concern will be with local ordinances, some types of businesses fall under state regulations. Food safety is a typical example. Before beginning any food business, check the state regulations carefully. Some border on the outrageous, requiring commercial stoves and refrigerators—even telling you how big they must be and what features they must have, even when your food product requires neither cooking nor refrigeration. Sometimes these requirements for a commercial kitchen apply only if you sell to stores, not if you sell directly to the consumer. But you need to know exactly what the state requires and if you need licensing to make a food product.

It's a good idea to hire a lawyer to make these inquiries; the benefits are many. First, the state inspections board doesn't get your name on their suspect list and second, a lawyer can quickly understand and interpret exactly what the law says and has access to cross-referencing of regulations from several different agencies which may be involved, as well as case law, which may have altered the enforcement.

The other issue you will need to know from the state is what taxes you are liable for. Some states have Business Profits or other taxes aimed at the self-employed.

But according to Barbara Radcliffe Rogers, most of your grief will come from the local government, and it is with them that you must deal the most directly. Before you even start, learn this vital rule: In small towns, policies often change when people change. What about the ordinances, you rightly ask, aren't they there to keep everything public and equal for everyone? Yes and no. Yes, there must be an ordinance, but much of the interpretation of these is left to appointed boards and committees who can make or break your operation. Simply because the selectman—who may also be the real estate agent intent on selling you the property—says there is no problem with the business you plan, doesn't mean you won't find trouble aplenty later when your plan goes before the Planning or Zoning Board—or even before the selectmen (I should note here that you can't assume that because this is the 90s, all towns—particularly in New England—have adopted the term Select*person*. Listen carefully to what locals call them and to what they call themselves. Even when they are female, they may be selectmen, and proud of it. If you plan to stay long in town, don't make gender bias in the language one of your pet campaigns. The selectmen will be there long after you are.)

Zoning

Be sure your land is zoned for business or at least that the town has a "cottage industry" rule. Find out what that allows. Does it allow another employee to work with you? Can customers come to your place of business? Be careful of ordinances that leave these details to the discretion of a board. And don't assume that since there has been a business on the property before that you are safe of "grandfathered." Read—and understand—the ordinances. Don't depend on anyone's opinion of what they mean or how they will be enforced, except that of a lawyer. And don't assume that because Sam down the road has a similar business the town allows, that you will be able to. Sam may be someone's brother.

Taxes

Will your property be taxed on a different basis if you start a business there? Are non-residential buildings taxed at a different rate? Are there permit fees?

Future plans

If your business is clearly a cottage industry, such as a potter who sells work at craft shows and in galleries, you will probably have little or no problem. But what if you decide to expand? Will you be able to or will you have to choose between expanding and staying where you are? What if you need to hire someone or decide to have a small retail shop?

Expansion

In order to build a new studio or bring in an employee to pack and ship your goods or tend the shop while you work, or in order to widen your driveway to accommodate the UPS truck, you may have to go before a town board. This will mean a hearing to which all your abutting neighbors will be invited to speak their piece. This makes it very important to be and stay on good terms with neighbors and to keep them informed, through casual conversation, social occasions and personal contact, exactly what you do and plan to do. You simply cannot believe the kinds of things neighbors will say at these meetings. Our neighbor wanted to add a bathroom to his studio and a neighbor ranted on at great length about the factory smokestacks that would soon fill our valley if this guitarmaker were allowed to expand. All for a loo!

Talk to others

Look around town and find other people with home businesses. Ask them directly how much grief the town gives them. The general attitude towards home businesses is not likely to change dramatically, so this information will let you know what the climate is.

Be upfront

At least to a degree. Don't ever assume that what they don't see won't concern them. Word moves fast in a small town and there is nothing that angers local officials more than thinking they've been deceived. There is no point in making enemies needlessly. if the ordinances require certain things of a business located there, and if you don't comply, you will be discovered sooner or later. You will either be fined, closed down, or discover that when you need to go to the town later they will remember quite clearly that you tried to get away with something earlier.

Moving Your Existing Business to the Country

Most people dream of starting their own businesses in a rural area, but if you're already operating your own business—and have it pretty well established—the odds are good that you'll have an easier time moving your business than a person who plans to move to the country and then either start one from scratch or buy an existing business.

There are certain standards that remain the same for both service and product-oriented businesses, but where the differences really begin to set you apart when you move to the country is whether you conduct business on a local or national basis. If it's the latter, it will be easier to move and re-establish yourself since you already probably do a lot of your business through the mail, phone, fax, and Federal Express. If the former, it will be harder, and your eventual success will depend on your local market and if your business is suitable for the surrounding area.

In some cases, some business won't translate successfully in the country. For instance, some businesses—like a dogwalking service—you might as well leave behind in the city. However, you can translate this to a pet-sitting service in the country, if there is a sizable community of people there who travel frequently.

The first thing you should do is check the Yellow Pages and the Business Services directory of the local newspaper to see how many competing businesses there are in your field, and if you think that the surrounding community would need one more. Call the people who will refer business to you—in the case of a pet-sitting service, contact local veterinarians; or, for instance, if you run a desktop publishing business, ask at the local print shops to get an idea of how your business would do. If there already are a number of similar businesses, then find out what niche is not being served and do some more digging to discover if the market is there.

If you find that your local-oriented business won't translate to the country, I'd suggest that you scrap it and start another business from scratch. Or, if you have a number of employees and are able to run the administrative side of the business from afar, then you might give this a try. This tends to work best for product-oriented businesses. With a service business, it's too easy for the quality of service to go down the tubes if you're not around. And unless you have an iron-hand manager—and sometimes even with a long-time employee, you can't be too sure of how they'll manage the office once you're out of sight—then running a business as an absentee owner can be very risky indeed.

If you already have a home-based cottage business and you're the sole employee, the move will be easy. All you have to do is send out change of address cards, load the moving van, and go. This, of course, is the big advantage to working for yourself and not having any employees. A warning, however: you may have some clients who will drop by the wayside because they may automatically assume that you're out of touch with the real world once you move to a rural area. However, while this was true when I moved to the country back in 1988, the six years that have elapsed since then have made a huge difference in the public's perception that anyone is able to run a business from anywhere, what with fax machines, modems, the Internet, and Federal Express pickups. Today, most people do realize that the location of your business is not what matters, it's your business itself.

If you're scouting out a particular area, the first thing you should do is to contact the local chamber of commerce in the town, county and state where you want to relocate your business. Contact all of them because they'll each give you a different perspective on the area's economic activity and outlook, and how it pertains to your business and the region as a whole. It's likely that your contact at each place will ask you if you'd like some assistance in your search, and—with your permission—will pass your name along to realtors, other business owners in the area, and suppliers.

Many chambers of commerce have sunk a lot of money into their economic development divisions in the form of ads in business magazines, promotional material, detailed research studies that point out the benefit of moving your business to their area, and even subsidized travel expenses for business prospects. They do this because they know if you move a business to their area, a number of things will happen: Even if you're a one-person operation, you'll help to increase the revenues of other businesses around you, which adds up to those magic words more jobs. And if you need to hire employees once you move to the area, the chamber of commerce will bend over backwards to help you find qualified candidates.

You'll also add cachet to the area and add to its image as a good place for small business to be and thrive. Chamber of Commerce directors and boards have been following these electronic business trends even more closely. They know that the future growth of their rural area will depend on their ability to attract small and even microscopic one-person businesses to their area. Because except for a few lucky beneficiaries, like the town in Kentucky that recently received a new customer service plant for the mammoth Boston-based Fidelity Investment Corporation, most rural development commissions realize that bringing a business this size to town is akin to winning the lottery, so they'll concentrate on attracting small businesses. Besides, it's much easier to court you and your enterprise than to go after huge corporations. And they know that huge businesses will radically change the character of local life, anyway.

So from the time that you make your initial inquiry, you can expect the red carpet to be rolled out for you and your business. You can also use this as leverage in order to get the things you need to insure a smooth transition into the area.

For instance, when you get a chamber of commerce representative on the phone, ask for the person who's in charge of attracting new business and feel free to bend her ear. Ask every question you can think of, and then some. Again, these people are paid to be helpful and lure newcomers—especially newcomers with their own businesses—to the area. And I've found them to be inordinately patient and helpful. In many cases, she will be your first business contact and sometimes the first contact that you'll have in the area at all, and she knows she'll earn brownie points if she can throw enough goodies your way to convince you to move.

Another good source of advice is a realtor, since if you do pick his area, this means that he'll earn a commission on your decision. And she may even be a better source of information about the community than the chamber of commerce rep, since he is probably out and talking with the other members of the local business community every day, whereas the chamber of commerce rep may not be as involved, at least those who work on a regional or state level.

And yet another good source of information about the prospects for moving your business to a rural area is the local Small Business Development Center—a branch of the Small Business Administration—in your chosen area. They offer networking opportunities, workshops and seminars, and one-on-one counseling sessions with local businesspeople, which would be a wonderful way for you to find out all of the nitty gritty about the area.

One thing you will want to check before you move to a rural area is the zoning, which is especially important if you want to run your business from home. Here, a real estate agent can be helpful, but not always. With a home business, you should find out about any provisions or restrictions that may apply to your particular business and the house and land that you want to rent or buy. And be careful: even though the previous owner may have run a home business in the same place, he may actually have been in violation of the local zoning ordinance for years but because he was related to one of the selectmen, the town decided not to enforce it, and decided to look the other way.

But now you come along, a newcomer, and they don't know you or anything about your business. Even if you describe your business in detail to them, they may not get it and decide to watch you like a hawk. Then, with the first tiny infraction, whether real or imagined, they'll be all over you like a cheap suit with a variety of fines, unnecessary permits, and other costs of doing business, all because they believe that you weren't totally upfront with them from the beginning. And you may well have been, but you weren't familiar enough with the ins and outs of running a rural business that there were definitely going to be some things that you weren't aware of.

Sorry, but as is the case with the Internal Revenue Service, ignorance will be no excuse. I know of a person in southwestern New Hampshire who had to move his home business out of his house because of some perceived insult he made to one of the selectmen's daughters. For 20 years, the town allowed him to run his business in a residential area, but one day, they decided to go after him. Even if a home-based business is grandfathered into the local laws, that means it could expire with you, so be careful and listen to what the town clerk and other local government authorities tell you to do.

If you have employees, of course you should offer them the choice of moving with you. Some may refuse, while others will welcome the opportunity to escape the city and be reassured of having a guaranteed job when they move. This will also streamline things for your own transition, since you don't have to spend the time or money to train somebody new.

However, there is one thing you should be aware of when taking your employees with you: in most cases, the wages in urban areas are higher than in rural areas, and if you take your employees with you, they'll expect their same urban pay in the country, even though their living expenses will probably be lower. If you start fresh with new employees in your new home, yes, you'll have to spend money training them, but you'll most likely be paying them a lower salary, which leaves you with more money to invest in your business. So it's totally your call.

Here are some steps you can take to ensure your own success once you move to a rural area:

♦ Once there, get involved in the local community. Sponsor a Little

League team, donate your products or services to a local community-based auction, and volunteer your business at other local events.

♦ Network, network, network. Join the chamber of commerce and attend the meetings. Follow up with business lunches, drop by other members' businesses, and use the services of other members. This is one of the best ways to fit into a new community.

♦ Pass along any extra business to other similar companies in town. This is a great way to cement future business relationships, and they'll do the same for you in the future.

♦ Allow yourself about a month to make the move. Once you know your moving date, send out change of address cards to all of your steady customers and invite them to call you personally with any questions or concerns that they may have. Send announcements to your new local press about your impending move. You may even start to hear from other business owners in the area as well as from prospective employees and independent contractors about job opportunities even before you move, so be forewarned.

♦ A month after you've moved, schedule an open house for members of the community and other business owners. Offer free refreshments and samples of your product. Send a press release to the local paper announcing the event and try to get on a few radio shows. You may also want to send invitations to other members of the chamber of commerce. Again, the directors and community liaisons will help you with the planning.

In the end, you'll find that running a business in the country will probably result in greater productivity and efficiency as you save hours of time each week waiting on line at the bank alone.

How *I* Moved My Business to the Country: One Person's Story

Phyllis and Cory Cohen were running their established animal behavior business in Garnerville, New York, when they decided to move to Sutton, Vermont, in the Northeast Kingdom section of the state. Here's what she has to say about the experience.

Q: Why did you pick Sutton, Vermont?

A: In 1991, my husband Cory and I spent our honeymoon in Lower Waterford, Vermont, in the Northeast Kingdom. We knew a honeymoon was supposed to be fantasy, but it was such a fantasy we just couldn't imagine what it would be like to live there. Over the years we started to think about how it could be a reality. When we visited in March of 1995 to stay at another B&B in the area, we just said let's do it, let's move no matter what. It's the kind of place to raise a family—we have two children—and we'll manage. We just have to find out how to do it, but we know this is where we want to be.

Q: How did you plan your move?

A: I say you just have to plunge right in and do it. If you speculate and talk too much about it, you just never get anywhere. We put our house on the market when we came back from that weekend in March. Within one week we had sold our house—we had placed it on the market at a fairly low price because we knew we wanted to get out—and two months later we were living up here. We put an offer on a house we had saw up here, and it was accepted.

Q: What about work?

A: We have an animal behavior business in Rockland County, New York that we still have. My husband commutes half the week to Rockland County for the business, and spends the other half up here. This was a bit of a sacrifice, since we have young children, but we figured doing it this way we could gain some momentum and still be where we want to be. Our business is training animals; we help people with their dog and cat problems. We've already made some contacts up here with vets, and they seem interested, but we need to make compromises. We need to modify the prices we charge and the way that we do business. In fact, everything is completely different here, but you have to be accommodating if you want to make a change.

We thought it would take a year before we were both living up here full time but now I think it will take a little longer to make the transition. It's affected by a lot of little things. The fact that we have small children makes us think about how we're going to plan all this. I'm distracted, obviously, but it's okay. The tradeoff is worth it because when Cory's here, he's really here. We have sheep now and he enjoys working on the house. It's such a nice contrast that it almost makes the commute worth it.

We also have to accommodate different types of pet problems up here. People in New York have problems with dogs that are inside a lot. Here, their dogs are outside most of the time. The problems we address here are more aggression-related.

The need to branch out to offer more services is the biggest thing on our minds right now. We're thinking about putting together some kind of publication. We feel we need to wear many hats. Cory has some ideas for pet-related products we might make, and we're considering raising goats. We have many ideas in our minds; we just have to have the time to implement them. You can't just rely on one thing, most people out here have a million different things they do. Spinning many plates is more fun anyway, and we don't have to rely on one thing either.

Q: How have people in Vermont treated you?

A: They've accepted us up here. I find that my children are a great common denominator in terms of making friends. I have tried very hard to be open minded to the differences, because people do things differently up here. They're less pretentious up here: wearing makeup and having your nails done is not important. I don't have to worry about what I look like, it's how I feel about how I look, and everybody else is the same way. I admit I wasn't like that back in New York. I found that there was a lot of keeping up with the Joneses there that I don't have to worry about here, and I feel so much better about that.

Q: What do you miss?

A: I miss shopping. It's not easy and it's not competitive because there's no one to compete with. You're paying higher prices for food and things like that, but I've found great consignment shops. And I've also discovered mail-order shopping.

Q: How have your budget and expenses changed?

A: The cost of living is hard to determine because we haven't lived through a winter yet. So far, our mortgage went down over $1000 a month, but we didn't make any money on the sale of our house in New York. Our property taxes have gone down: I had a fifth of an acre in New York, now I have eight acres, but I'm paying a third of the property taxes I was paying in New York. Our revenue has decreased 10 percent from before since Cory's not working as much as before.

Q: What has surprised you most about rural life?

A: What's surprised me most is the number of power outages. We had 24 hours of nothing last week, since everything is operated by electricity except the woodstove. But I'm also surprised at how happy I can be in such a rural area. I'm a city girl and I never thought I could adjust as well as I have. If you just let it happen to you, you forget where you're from, and I'm very pleased at the way I've adapted. And people are wonderful out here, which never ceases to amaze me because I have a bit of a skeptical eye, being from a big city.

Q: What advice do you have for people who want to move their businesses to the country?

A: If you're going to take the plunge, you have to make sure you're comfortable with a more rural environment. I don't suggest dwelling on it, I don't suggest planning it for a year. If you're going to put your house on the market, do it quick and accept a price fairly quickly because you're going to save money on your mortgage payments anyway. Just do it and do it quickly, especially if you have a family, because time is too precious. The sooner you make the move the less you're thinking about making the move. I think that's the best thing that we did.

Visiting B&Bs and talking to the waiters in the dining rooms and to the owners of B&Bs also helped us with what to expect. If you happen to be lucky enough to talk to people who used to come from a city, it's sometimes easier to talk to them to see how they made the transition. Stand in front of the supermarket and see who goes in and out. That's a great indication.

Before You Buy A Country Business

If you dream of having a small business to run out of your country home, you'd better look carefully before you choose a location. Not all land or locations are right for all businesses, and however small you may expect your enterprise to be, it will require some specifics from its location. So while you are shopping for a house or for land on which to build one, consider some of the following questions. And if you're not planning to run a home-based business, some of these issues will spark questions if you are going to work for somebody else when you move to the country. For instance, do you really want to be that far away from the main drag?

♦ What kind of business do you plan to open? Even if you don't have a particular enterprise in mind, you probably know a little about your choices. Do you plan to have customers or clients come to you, or will most of your business be conducted through the mail and over the phone?

♦ Do you plan a retail business where several people might come at once or one where clients will make an appointment? Each type of business presents its own unique challenges and if you have narrowed your scope a little you will know which questions to concentrate on.

♦ Is the property easy for customers to get to? Is it on a well-traveled road where passersby will see your sign? Is it easy to give directions to? Does the road provide good access in all seasons? Is the driveway accessible in the winter? Even if clients don't need to get in, can the UPS truck or other suppliers? In the wintertime, the UPS truck can't make it up my driveway-from-hell, so he drops my packages off at one of the general stores in town.

♦ Can you put up signs directing people to your business? Don't take this for granted. In Vermont, for example, businesses are allowed only two directional signs, so those which require several turns between the main road and their driveway may not be able to lead customers there with signs. What is the local sign ordinance? Can you even put a sign at your own entrance or on your house?

♦ If you are not on a well-traveled road, are you close to some other business that draws customers? Can you "tag along," giving directions such as "just past Pete's Barbecue"?

♦ Once customers arrive, where will they park cars? Nearly any town requires that customers not park on the road. Issues such as the visibility in either direction, width of the available entrance road, and terrain will have to be addressed—by you, if not by the town board that gives you a permit to open shop. Is there room for several cars at one time or will you have to grade the land to make room?

♦ Do you have room to expand? Although you may begin as a tiny home business, your idea may prove a goldmine and you may need added sales area, storage space or workshop. Is there room for these or will you have to move in order to grow?

♦ Is the land "right" for the business you envision? If, for example, you picture a charming B&B in the country, do the surroundings fit the picture? Does the farm across the road add to the scenic atmosphere or to the smell in the air? Does Fred's Auto Body Shop face your quaint sign? If you plan a farm or garden related business will the land support it or is it a sandpit in disguise? Will guests be able to have tea on the terrace or will mosquitoes breeding in the nearby swamp drive them away?

♦ In this electronic age, how far are you from the information superhighway? For instance, is the property served by a small private telephone company that cannot provide you with needed services? Does AOL or a local Internet service provider have a local access number, or will your online time be at toll-call rates?

♦ Do snow, ice, or wind frequently cause tree limbs to fall on power lines? Neighbors can tell you how often the power goes out, a major consideration if you depend on a computer or fax.

♦ How close are you to the nearest post office? Are you on a rural route where the mail carrier can bring you stamps? Will they deliver packages too big for the roadside box or do you have to go to the post office to get them? Can you get a post office box? Many smaller stations have a long waiting list for these.

♦ Where is the UPS or Federal Express office? Will the courier services pick up at your location or do you have to go to them? Do they provide morning delivery for overnight packages? Don't assume this service once you move to the country; ask specific questions.

If the rural business that you plan to start does not depend on clients doing business in person, you may not need to worry about some of these issues, but others may create unique problems.

Country Business Profile
General Store

Westport General Store
Bob and Lorraine Caristi
Westport Island, Maine

Description of Business

A convenience store geared toward a rural community serving both locals and tourists.

Ease of Startup

Difficult. If you start from scratch, you'll need to renovate and set up accounts with suppliers. It is easier to buy an existing business.

Range of Initial Investment

$200,000-$400,000 for inventory and building, which usually includes owner's quarters.

Time Commitment

Full-time

Can You Run the Business From Home?

You should live upstairs or nearby.

You should live upstairs or nearby.

Success Potential

Moderate. The larger variety of products you carry and the more centrally located the store, the higher the success rate.

How to Market the Business

Carry a large selection of products at reasonable prices and provide good service. Advertising and other promotion won't bring in new people if they have to drive any distance.

The Pros

When you're the only store in town, you're important to the community.

The Cons

The hours are long and the work is physically hard.

Special Considerations

Owning a general store is one of the top three businesses people dream of, mostly to escape the city. In each of these businesses—innkeeping and gift shops are the other two—the dream does not even begin to match the hard work of the reality.

For More Information

National Grocers Association, 1825 Samuel Morse Drive. Reston, VA 22090.

Story of the Business

Listen to how Bob Caristi describes the difference between his corporate job—which he left to move up to Maine with his wife, Lorraine and their general store, which opened for business in June 1992:

"At my corporate job, I seldom put in 40 hours," he relates. "Here, we work untold hours for relatively little money, but the compensation is in a different form; we're no longer being paid in dollars. Anyone thinking about doing what we did better realize you have to do everything yourself. Most people tend not to know what that's like. It also takes a tremendous range of talents to do this: you have to be bookkeeper and businessperson, personable, physically strong and willing and able to work long hours."

Undoubtedly, many of the people who come to the Westport General Store in the summertime are in the very position that Bob hated enough to leave and envy his new career. It may look easy, but running a general store after the age of 50 is a daunting experience, especially if you choose not to hire help, like Bob and Lorraine.

They sat down one day back in Massachusetts and realized they both wanted to leave their jobs. They asked themselves the question, "How do you do what you're good at, get away from what you don't like, live where you want and yet somehow make a living?" They decided their skills were complementary—Lorraine is more people-oriented, while Bob likes to deal with tangible objects and manufacturers.

They put it all together and decided to open a mom-and-pop store on the coast of Maine. "I handle the business and mechanics, and she primarily deals with people," explains Bob. "This type of business is such that unless you're an idiot, you're going to make money from the beginning."

They started saving for the purchase in 1986 and bought the store in 1991 while they were still working in Massachusetts. They saved enough to buy the store outright to avoid the pressure of a mortgage. They finally moved to Maine in April 1992. They spent two months fixing up the store and opened for business at the end of June.

The store is 1,500 square feet. They carry beer and wine, canned goods, bread and dairy products. The Caristis also have an extensive grocery line, which most general stores don't do. When they first opened, they guessed at what they should sell. In the year and a half they've been open, they have chosen new products according to the demand that comes from two distinct communities: locals and the summer residents.

"There are two Westports," explains Bob, "and there are fundamental differences in the nature of the two." For instance, the summer residents want bottled water and antifreeze for their toilets and sinks at the end of the season. The year-round people want other things.

"Your customers are your boss, which can be trying at times, but the minute you forget that, you're out of business," he warns. "It's nice to be a central point in the town and to have people rely on us to provide services and products."

Unlike other nearby general stores, the Caristis have deliberately chosen to limit their product line. "There's a lot of call for the lottery, but even though it has a significant impact on gross, we don't want to do it because it's a pain in the butt," he remarks. "We also don't want to sell prepared food and sandwiches because of the potential for waste of perishable items."

They also refuse to have employees; this makes for some very long days and nights. Besides not having to pay high rates for worker's compensation in addition to payroll taxes, Bob says he does it himself because no employee cares like he does. "Especially with a new business and with this kind of business, I want to make sure that customers are being appropriately served. There's also no pilferage and no errors."

His marketing campaign consists of being pleasant to people, carrying the merchandise that people want and being impeccably honest and service-oriented. "You're only going to attract people within a convenient driving distance, so if you do things right, you're going to maximize the draw within the geographic area," he explains.

They didn't know anything about running a general store when they started, but they thought they could translate what they knew into a viable business, and they have. "We did it with intelligence and guts."

Country Business Profile
Llama Raising

Pleasant Bay Llama Keep
Joan Yeaton
Addison, Maine

Description of Business

Llamas are a popular, versatile animal that require a minimum of attention. You can sell their fleece, use males for stud service, sell young llamas and breed females or use them for trekking.

Ease of Startup

Moderate. If you already have sufficient land—three to four llamas per acre is average—you need to buy the llamas and build a shelter.

Range of Initial Investment

$100,000 if you already have the land.

Time Commitment

Full-time

Can You Run the Business From Home?

Yes

Success Potential

Moderate. The bigger the herd, the better. This allows you to concentrate on more than one specialty.

How to Market the Business

Advertising, brochures, word of mouth, agricultural shows and fairs.

The Pros

Llamas are intelligent, loving animals—they only spit at each other.

The Cons

Llamas range from $500 to $5,000 for males and from $4,000 to $11,000 for females. Fancy llamas can cost $50,000. With high prices on a nonessential item, your income can be sporadic.

Special Considerations

Most people aren't familiar with llamas; llama breeders and sellers have to act as ambassadors to the public.

For More Information

International Llama Association, 2755 Locust Street, Suite 114, Denver, CO 80222; 303-7569004; *Llama Banner Magazine*, 714 Poyntz, Suite B, Box 1968, Manhattan, KS 66502.

Story of the Business

Joan Yeaton and her husband, Lee, were living in Exeter, New Hampshire. He had an insurance agency, and she had a real estate firm, 10 llamas and not enough time for any of it.

"Wouldn't it be nice," they thought one day, "to have enough time to enjoy them and not have to go to an office?" They began to think about how they could pull this off. Before they knew it, the Yeatons had sold everything except their llamas and furniture and were building a house on the seacoast of Maine, less than an hour from the Canadian border.

Joan had been exposed to llamas when she was in Peru years earlier, and she fell in love with them. "I loved the idea of raising llamas because I didn't have to slaughter or eat what I raised in order to make a living from it," she says. "Because you don't have to kill them, you can put a huge emotional investment in them, and it pays off."

In Exeter, she started with two animals and grew from there. Today she has around 30 llamas at any time; 15 to 19 of them breeding females. People bring their llamas to the Yeaton's farm to be bred; stud fees range from $600 to $1,000.

Joan sells females and males; their prices depend on their color and blood lines. Young males go from $500 to $1,500, while proven males—those who have fathered—sell for $2,000 to $5,000. Females that haven't given birth cost $4,000 to $5,000; Joan sells topflight bred females—sold when they are pregnant—for up to $11,000.

She guarantees a live birth with her bred females. If the baby dies, she will breed the mother again for the customer for no charge. The Yeatons chose to specialize in selling llamas in the $5000 to

$10,000 range because they didn't have the money to invest in expensive llamas. They also thought there would be more demand for moderately priced llamas. "We were targeting people like ourselves," remarks Joan.

Joan also runs a three-room bed and breakfast out of her home that looks out onto Pleasant Bay and says she frequently sells llamas to guests who visit the B & B. "Many come to the B & B not knowing what to expect from the llamas, but they'll go out for a walk with the llamas and come back a convert," she reports. "We just sold a llama to people who came to the B & B four years ago. It's amazing how something I did a few years ago will come to fruition. In a business like this, you're in it for the long haul, since the lifespan of a llama can range from 15 to 30 years."

Though there are more people raising llamas today than when she started in 1988, the prices have leveled off. This has allowed many people to buy llamas who couldn't afford it previously.

Joan advises people who are interested in raising llamas to start slowly and expect to work hard. Some weeks she works 35 hours. She spends several hours a day with the llamas; then she does peripheral things like working in the barn and mending fencing. On some days she spends all day with the animals.

She suggests people visit a variety of llama farms to pick the style that would fit them best. "It depends on what you think you can live on," she indicates. "If we thought we needed $100,000 a year to live on, we wouldn't be able to support ourselves. Instead we sold our businesses, took a low mortgage and planned to live relatively simply. We put our money into the buildings and increasing the herd." The Yeatons also grow their own food and try to be as self-sufficient as possible.

Besides the B & B, potential customers find out about Pleasant Bay through advertisements in local papers and local trade publications, but most of their business comes through word of mouth and referrals. Maine has its own association for llama breeders, which has 35 members. They meet for a potluck supper several times a year, sharing stories and advice. The group also has a field day every June where the general public is invited; thousands of people attend.

The Yeatons gross anywhere from $20,000 to $35,000 a year from their breeding services. "You can't expect to make a killing in llamas," advises Joan. "we look at it as more of a lifestyle."

Chapter Two

What You Need For Your Country Business

Before you proceed to plan your country business, it's a good idea to take some time to evaluate yourself, your financial situation, and the venue you plan to use. Doing your homework at this stage will save you from making big and possibly costly mistakes down the road.

Assessing Your Personal Goals

First, you must determine what your overall personal goals are and how starting and running a country business fits in with them.

Take some time to answer the following questions in detail:

♦ What are the three main reasons why you want to open a country business?

- How long to you plan to run the country business?

- Do you see your country business as a hobby or a full-time business?

- What are your personal goals aside from your country business? Do you plan to retire at a certain age, or move on to something else after running the business for ten years?

If you've ever run your own business, then you already know the hard work involved. If you haven't, let this serve as a warning that you'll probably be spending more hours working than you realize.

Some people view a country business as a way they can go into semi- or early retirement, or the only way they can finally move to the country and be able to make a decent living. Other people dream of the self-sufficiency they'll achieve by running their own business.

A country business is like any other business: You need it to provide income along with a healthy dose of satisfaction. You also need to have something in your life besides the business. That's why it's important to set goals for yourself that are totally separate from the business. Burnout is very common when you run your own business, and one way to prevent it is to plan your goals in advance, whether you want to raise some animals or spend more time with your friends and family. After all, if you want to move to the country, you're looking for a total lifestyle change, and not just to change the way you make a buck.

Assessing Your Financial Goals

If you want to get rich, go buy a book by Charles Givens. If you want to have a decent income while you build equity and increase your revenues a little bit each year, then keep reading.

To see if your financial goals jive with running a country business, ask yourself the following questions:

- What would you rather have after ten years of hard work: A large sum of money in the bank, or equity in a valuable home and business which would be relatively easy to sell?

- What's the least amount of money you could live on each month, provided that the mortgage, taxes, and utilities are paid for?

- Do you like doing just one thing to make a living, or do you prefer to juggle a variety of tasks?

For most people who decide to start their own country business, money is of secondary concern. Of course, it takes money to get started, but most people who start a country business are looking for the lifestyle first and income second. These priorities will help keep you motivated during the slow times.

After the ups and downs that were driving the first year of any business, it will seem like you can relax a little as your revenue becomes a little bit more predictable, but you'll still find it necessary to reinvest much of the money back into the business in order to keep your revenue growing. Because of this, unless you have a trust fund or a sizable side income, you must learn to live frugally, at least for awhile. In time, most rural entrepreneurs learn to view this aspect of the business as a benefit, as their country business provides them with a lifestyle and experience that they couldn't get any other way. Even though you may be working twice as hard running a country business as anything you've done before, most people say they wouldn't trade it in for their previous lives for any amount of money.

Assessing Your Risk Tolerance

Many people who dream of opening a country business love the idea and constantly fantasize about it, but when it comes right down to it, most will never take the necessary steps because they're reluctant to leave the security of having a regular job, health insurance, the familiarity of a particular lifestyle—you name it—even if they're unhappy in their current lives.

A person who falls into this category has a low tolerance for risk of any kind.

On the other hand, a person who can tolerate risk, who even welcomes it to some degree, recognizes that even though he may do everything necessary to operate and promote his business successfully, there is still some element of risk to the business that he will be unable to control, like economic downturns and fickle weather. He accepts this as a normal part of doing business, and proceeds accordingly.

What's your tolerance for risk? Find out by answering the following questions:

♦ Have you ever run a business of your own before? If so, how did you react when things slowed down? If you don't have experience in running a business, how do you think you would react—with panic, or the ability to constantly keep the big picture in mind?

♦ How would you react if you or a family member had to spend a week in the hospital and you didn't have health insurance because you needed the money to pay the mortgage?

♦ How important is it to you to have material items to validate your self-worth? What would you do if you were to suddenly lose them?

People who don't have a high tolerance for risky situations often see the world in black and white, with no room for gray areas. Sure, the prospect of quitting your job and opening a country business and even moving to a new area is frightening even to people who like some excitement. There's no safety net; what makes you think you can pull this off; and what if you fail? are probably only three of the concerns that are running through your head before you decide to start your country business.

However, men and women who are able to see these factors as challenges to meet and surpass, and who like the absence of a schedule—as well as not knowing what the next day or week will bring—should be able to deal well with the unpredictable nature of the business.

And sometimes, in order to start your business and begin to live the kind of life that you love, it's necessary to do without the things you treasure. Many people finance their country businesses by selling family heirlooms, cars, even their homes, when there's no guarantee they'll be able to succeed.

If you place great importance on your possessions and hate the idea of essentially gambling with their value, you should think twice about starting your country business, start it with a pared-down version, or else find someone else to finance it.

Skill Requirements

Though many prospective rural entrepreneurs take a variety of seminars, work with consultants, and talk to other country businessowners before getting their business off the ground, the fact is that you will discover that you will call many different skills into play from the first day of business.

You'll need to learn about cash flow, bookkeeping, and marketing—and you'll learn about the basics in *The Complete Country Business Guide*—but most rural entrepreneurs usually learn as they go, and by asking other entrepreneurs what has worked best for them.

Even if you've never run a business before, you probably already know what you're good at from working for other people. And where your skills aren't as good, you'll be able to learn enough to get by. If you can afford to hire someone else to do the work, however, go ahead.

Attitude Requirements

The ideal rural entrepreneur is a person who's a cynical optimist, or, as some might say, an optimistic cynic. This is someone who has a positive attitude towards the world, but who also is not surprised when things go wrong. When that happens, you spring into action and do whatever it takes to address the problem and get everything back to normal—until another fire breaks out, that is.

Surprises are a regular occurrence in any business, especially the first few months. As long as you maintain a positive attitude and remain alert to problems that need your immediate attention while learning patience for those that can wait, you'll be able to run a successful country business and maintain your equilibrium as well. And remember, if you're running the business full-time, at least once a week you should make it a point to take some downtime for yourself, which will help you maintain your positive attitude as well.

Resources

The Small Business Administration
The Small Business Administration, which you help to pay for with your tax dollars, is a veritable gold mine of information if you want to become a rural entrepreneur.

There are three major divisions within the Small Business Administration that can assist you in the startup phase of your business, as well as provide you with advice and assistance once your business is up and running.

One is the Small Business Development Center, which counsels entrepreneurs in every conceivable type of business and at every level of development. The SBDC will set you up in private sessions with an entrepreneur who has experience running a business that's similar to yours. There, you can ask about any phase of running a country business that you'd like, from marketing to locating suitable financing and how to keep the business going in tough times.

The SBA also runs the Small Business Institute on a number of college campuses nationwide. Each SBI tends to specialize in a given field, from engineering to business management, but if you're looking for very specific information, contact the nearest SBI that has the program you want. The assistance at a SBI is largely provided by students in the program, but always under the watchful eye of a professor or administrator.

SCORE, or the Service Corps of Retired Executives, can be an exciting place for you to get information about your business. SCORE officers provide one-on-one counseling with retired businesspeople who volunteer their time to help entrepreneurs like you get the help you need. Each volunteer counselor has extensive experience in a particular field, and is eager to share his insights.

SCORE also offers a variety of seminars and workshops on all aspects of business ownership that aspiring rural entrepreneurs can also attend; here, you'll get specific advice about the nuts and bolts of running a business in general, from bookkeeping to taxes.

The Small Business Administration also has a program where it loans money to small businesses, but you have to apply through a bank. The SBA then kicks in some of the funds and serves to guarantee your loan based on your business plan. The SBA also offers a large variety of helpful booklets and brochures on all aspects of running a business.

To locate the SBA and its other programs, look in the white pages of the phone book under United States Government. Call the office nearest you for information about the programs and services they provide locally.

To contact the SBA in Washington directly, write to them at:

The Small Business Administration
409 Third Street SW
Washington DC 20416

To get in touch with the variety of services, call this number for immediate help:

SBA Answer Desk 800-827-5722

Organizations That Help Small Business

Once you start your country business, you'll be joining the millions of other Americans who are owning and operating their own small businesses. Specific questions can pop up, and you'll undoubtedly want to network with other entrepreneurs who aren't necessarily in the same field in order to get your questions answered.

There are a number of nationwide associations that provide small business owners with information, specific resources, discounts on business products and services, and the ability to work with other members. The government also gets into the act.

Here's a listing of a number of nationwide organizations that have proven to be valuable to the entrepreneurs who join them.

National Association for the Self-Employed
POB 612067
Dallas TX 75261
800-232-6273

National Association of Home Based Businesses
10451 Mill Run Circle
Suite 400
Owings Mills MD 21117
410-363-3698

National Federation of Independent Business
600 Maryland Ave SW
Suite 700
Washington DC 20024
202-554-9000

American Woman's Economic Development Corporation
71 Vanderbilt Avenue
Suite 320
New York NY 10169
800-222-2933

National Association of Women Business Owners
1377 K Street NW
Suite 637
Washington DC 20005
301-608-2590

National Minority Business Council
235 E 42 Street
New York NY 10017
212-573-2385

Country Business Profile
Antique Shop

The Country Loft
Lionel Carbonneau
South Barre, Vermont

Description of Business

A store that sells antiques and collectibles.

Ease of Startup

Moderate. It can take a few years to build up a diverse inventory of high-quality antiques.

Range of Initial Investment

$20,000 for inventory.

Time Commitment

Part-or full-time

Can You Run the Business From Home?

Yes

Success Potential

Difficult. The business is glutted, unscrupulous dealers and poor-quality inventory have caused people to cut back on their purchases.

How to Market the Business

Advertising, word of mouth, referrals, good location.

The Pros

If you love antiques, buying them for a store feels great. Running a shop is an enjoyable way to meet people, both locals and visitors.

The Cons

Good quality antiques are hard to find; competition drives up prices.

Special Considerations

Running an antique store is a dream country business for many people, but like all dream businesses, it's sometimes hard to see the reality.

For More Information

Antique Dealers' Association of America, Box 335, Green Farms, CT 06436; local and statewide associations. *The Upstart Guide to Owning and Managing an Antiques Business*, Lisa Rogak (Dover, NH: Upstart Publishing, 1994).

Story of the Business

Lionel Carbonneau is a patient man. When he and his wife, Marilyn, were married in 1948, they started to collect antiques, which they both loved. As the years went on, he wanted to get into the business, but with two daughters who Lionel wanted to put through college, his dream was postponed.

In 1972, he was ten years away from retirement, and he already knew what he wanted to do when he left his job. He started to build his inventory gradually, buying from individuals and knocking on doors. "Since I was in sales, I was used to that," he says.

In 1982 he finally retired, but he had to wait just a little longer. He and Marilyn decided to open the shop in a barn that was attached to an old house they had bought in central Vermont, one town over from the state capitol. Lionel needed to fix up the barn; he put in stairs so customers could get to the loft. Then he filled the barn with all of the antiques he had collected over the years.

In 1983 The Country Loft opened for business. The Country Loft specializes in primitives. Lionel says they sell a lot of rope beds. Local people make up most of his business, and they're familiar with the open "by chance or by appointment" policy of many businesses in northern New England that are located in unheated buildings. "We're not married to the business," indicates Lionel. "If we want to take a day off, we do." The $25,000 to $30,000 gross the shop brings in helps to pay the Carbonneaus' taxes and insurance.

Some of the same people who buy antiques from Lionel also sell items to him. "When we buy, we try to be fair with them on price," he remarks. "If I make a 25 to 30 percent markup on an item, I'm happy."

The most difficult part of the business is finding good merchandise for the shop. "I still go out and look for things," he says. "I also advertise in the paper saying that I'm looking to buy antiques. People call. They think they have an antique, but they don't. For every five items I see, I'll buy maybe one."

Marilyn waits on customers while Lionel is out scouting. "For a good retirement business, the spouse should be interested in the business," he believes. "My wife and I work together, and I think that's what makes a good business. I could see myself doing it on my own, but we do it better together."

Lionel does a little advertising in the local newspapers. He belongs to the statewide organization for antique dealers, but he says most of his customers are people who've dealt with him before.

Both he and his wife like meeting the people who come to the shop. He's amazed at the attitude of the people at some shops he's visited. "I've been places where I've walked in and the owner is grouchy," he reports. "That's not right. You can't expect that every person who comes in is going to buy something."

He suggests that people who are interested in starting an antique shop take their time. "Crawl before you walk," he advises. "You've got to know antiques; otherwise, you'll go out and get stung. You have to love it. I'm happy with what we're doing now; I don't want to get too big."

Country Business Profile
Boat Tour Company

Balmy Days Cruises
Diane and Bob Campbell
Boothbay Harbor, Maine

Description of Business

A company that offers excursions and transportation for tourists and residents via boat.

Ease of Startup

Difficult. You have to buy and equip a boat, get licensed and attract customers.

Range of Initial Investment

$50,000 and up.

Time Commitment

Full-time in season

Can You Run the Business From Home?

No

Success Potential

Moderate. Depending upon where you live, the business can be seasonal and very competitive.

How to Market the Business

Advertising, word of mouth, local tourist attractions, publicity.

The Pros

You're literally the captain of your own ship. You get paid to run a boat.

The Cons

The weather can determine your success.

Special Considerations

Running a boat tour operation will seem like heaven for people who love boats.

For More Information

National Association of Charterboat Operators, 655 15th Street NW, Suite 310, Washington DC 20005

Story of the Business

Diane and Bob Campbell were living in Massachusetts when a rare opportunity came their way. They had the chance to buy a couple of excursion boats on the coast of Maine. The Campbells had spent vacations sailing in Maine, and Bob had worked on a boat as a child. He had been friendly with a tour boat operator during the summers he spent in Maine. When he found out the boats were for sale, he approached the owner and bought them. As Diane put it, "It didn't take long to make up our minds."

The Balmy Days II serves as one of the ferries to Monhegan Island; the Maranbo II is the sole form of transportation to Squirrel Island, where many summer residents have their homes. The Balmy Days II can carry 150 passengers; it makes one trip a day to the island in season. It drops off and picks people up, and then returns to shore for a dinner cruise each night. The trip to Squirrel Island takes about an hour on the Maranbo II, which holds 69 passengers and makes from seven to eight trips a day.

When they bought the boats, Diane became the business manager in charge of sales and marketing. Bob took on the responsibility of running the boats and captaining them. Diane didn't know a thing about marketing and promotion when she started. She began by writing and designing a brochure that described the trips. She attended seminars and workshops sponsored by the Maine Publicity Bureau. Her membership in that group allowed her to place brochures in five tourist information booths throughout the state. "We advertised in several magazines and joined the local Chamber of Commerce," she relates. Diane also hangs signs on the booth for the boat and places brochures in local motels and hotels.

Their efforts worked well enough that they were able to add a sailboat called the Bay Lady, with a capacity of 15, to their fleet. Diane also runs a bed and breakfast called the Anchor Watch Inn year-round, though winters are pretty slow.

The total staff for all the boats comes to 14 for the full season. One of the benefits of running your own business is you can hire whomever you want. In the Campbells' case, that means family. "My father and my daughter work for us; my son is captain and operations manager in charge of the crew; his wife does the bookkeeping," says Diane. "The whole family is involved. It's a real pleasure to see the kids all the time in the summer and work together."

The biggest challenge the Campbells face is the weather. "It's the critical factor for success in any given year," indicates Diane. "If we have a good year weatherwise, it doesn't matter what's happening in the rest of the world, we'll have a good year. But if the weather's bad, it doesn't matter how great the economy is or how many Europeans are traveling in this country, we'll have a bad year."

The Balmy Days II runs every day from early June through September; it runs on weekends through Columbus Day. The Maranbo II runs year-round; in winter it runs three days a week for the two people who stay on the island as caretakers. The Campbells estimate they carry up to 7,000 passengers a year on their three boats.

"When people ask us if we like running our own business, I say we gave up our nine-to-five jobs for five-to-nine jobs," jokes Diane. "But there's no problem with that because we love what we do. We enjoy meeting so many interesting people. It's a short season, though, so the rest of the year we lead a more normal life."

Chapter Three

Planning Your Country Business

Planning is the key to the success of your country business. Without it is akin to setting out for a cross-country car trip without a map. You'll spend a good deal of time relying on the advice of other people to give you information on where to go and how to get there.

Take the time now to plan your business down to the smallest detail. It's the single most important thing you can do.

Planning to Succeed

Before starting a country business—or any business, for that matter—every rural entrepreneur expects to succeed. However, only a handful plan to succeed, and therein lies the difference.

Planning to succeed means you'll have to think about how you envision your country business, as well as writing a business plan and a marketing plan. Though many businesses do succeed without developing these planning materials, it's easier to succeed if you do take the time to plot out every aspect of your business, from the magazines you'd like to advertise in to the pictures you'll hang on the walls.

Getting the details down in writing months—or years—before your first customer shows up not only helps to clarify your vision, but also provides you with a blueprint so you can check every so often to see that you're on target and on schedule. Take the time now to plan your business. Later on, it may be too late and lead to...

Unplanned Failure

Even with the best of intentions and the most detailed business and marketing plans, sometimes a country business will fail, or at least seriously underperform the owners' initial projections. Perhaps the owners' expectations were overly optimistic and their budget didn't allow for much leeway. And sometimes events beyond their control can occur—like a prolonged downturn in the economy or a sharp decrease in the market's demand for your product or service—and they won't be able to salvage even a well-done business plan.

The two most common causes of unplanned failure are lack of capital and not enough marketing. I say unplanned, because even though most business and marketing plans do account for these factors, most people underestimate the amount of cash they'll need to pay the bills during slow times, and the time they'll need to spend on marketing just to get their names out there, and then keep them there. Another little-mentioned reason why country businesses fail is because despite everything they read and all the workshops and seminars that they tend to vastly underestimate the amount of time and energy that running their own business requires. This is especially true for couples who run the business together; they may be surprised at the wedge the business can begin to drive into their relationship if they're not careful. And if they have different management styles that they weren't aware of way back when they first decided to start the business, then watch out.

As you're drawing up the three major ways to avoid unplanned failure—envisioning your country business, writing a business plan, and writing a marketing plan—keep aware of anything that causes little alarms to go off in your brain, like keeping only $1000 in an emergency fund account, you're right to stop, take a deep breath, and go for a walk. Listen to these warning signals and try to put some perspective into what it's like to run a country business before you even start.

The best way to avoid unplanned failure is if you can regard all income from the country business as additional income, or else as money to plow back into the business, and not revenue you have to depend on to pay the mortgage and taxes. Of course, that means you might have to start slowly while you and/or your partner continue to work at a full-time job, but many experienced rural entrepreneurs suggest that you start slow and then slowly expand the business. That way, the mistakes you make will still be manageable, and you won't freak out when a big bill comes along, because you'll still have income and some savings.

Envisioning Your Country Business

Before you get into the nuts and bolts of writing a business and marketing plan for your country business, now is a perfect time to fantasize about how you see your new life as a rural entrepreneur. What will your schedule look like? Who will be your first customers?

You may want to fill out this form twice: once for how your country business will appear in the beginning, and again a year or more later, after you have some perspective and experience.

If you're opening your country business with a partner, both of you should separately fill out this form and compare your answers. If any of your answers are radically different, you should address them now to avoid unnecessary expense and disagreements later.

♦ What would you like the name of your country business to be?

♦ How many different products and/or services will you offer?

♦ What will be the tone you want to convey to your customers: calm, expensive, chaotic, experienced?

♦ What will your office look like?

♦ What kind of sign will you hang out front, if indeed you need to hang a sign at all?

♦ What other touches do you want to add that will make your country business one that will keep your customers coming back?

♦ What's important to you when you visit a business that's similar?

And so on. Try to incorporate these factors into your own vision.

Writing Your Business Plan

Why should you have a business plan? You know exactly what you're going to do—start a country business—and where it will be located as well as the target date for your first day of business. And even if your goals are not that specific at this point, you probably have an idea of the type of country business you'd like to run.

Writing a business plan will help you to map out a specific blueprint for you to follow on your way to meeting your goals. A business plan ensures that there is no question about the smallest aspect of starting your country business; in the confusion and excitement of planning your business, after all, many things get overlooked. Getting everything down in writing provides you not only with a checklist but also a detailed itinerary. And since you write the plan yourself, you'll be able to tailor it to your own needs, and also to tinker with it later when unforeseen roadblocks begin to emerge.

With a business plan in hand, you'll be able to show the bank, your suppliers, and other potential business contacts exactly how you envision your country business, in language and figures they understand. But writing is a funny thing that reveals a lot as it unfolds. Not only will your business plan provide you with a broad picture of your business, in addition to allowing you to get all of the little details down in writing, but you'll also think of other things as you think, write, and plan aspects of your prospective business that might not have occurred to you otherwise.

Having a business plan written before you do anything else for your country business will put you way ahead of your competition, since most entrepreneurs—rural or otherwise—do not take the time before hand to plan out their strategies so carefully.

Although a business plan is vital to the successful startup of a country business, it is meant to be used and referred to as you go. Periodically checking the progress you're making against the goals you put forth in the plan allow you to see where changes need to be made, as well as seeing whether you're keeping up with, or even surpassing, your original goals.

One of the top reasons why businesses fail is due to a lack of planning. Writing a detailed business plan that is geared towards the type of country business you wish to open will let you see if your goals fit in with your budget, if you should wait until you've raised more money, or indeed, if this is the right business for you after all.

Anyone who reads your business plan will be able to get a clear picture of the type of country business you'd like to run, as well as its projected financial health. Spend the time now on it; if you run into trouble later on and don't have a business plan to refer back to, it just might be too late.

Sample Business Plan

A business plan can be only a few pages long, or a massive 100-page document that maps out every single detail involved in running your country business.

Though it takes more time, it's best to err on the side of quantity when writing a business plan for your country business. The more you know about your business before you talk to your first customer, the better prepared you will be for the surprises that will inevitably arise.

A business plan should have five sections: A cover sheet, your statement of purpose for the country business, and a table of contents. Then, the meaty part: *Section One* describes the business: What you provide, your target markets, your location, competition, and personnel you expect to hire. *Section Two* concerns financial information about your country business: Income and cash flow projections, and if you're buying a country business from another owner, the financial history of the business as they ran it.

Another section of your business plan should consist of supporting documents that back up the information you're providing in the other sections. A resume of your employment history, your credit report, letters of reference, and any other items you believe will help the reader to better grasp what you are striving to do with your country business.

Here's a sample business plan for a rural B&B that a young professional couple is planning to buy:

The Berry Patch Bed & Breakfast

Blueberry Hill

Canterbury, New Hampshire 03333

603-987-6543

A Business Plan by Carol & Richard Jamm

Statement of Purpose

This business plan will serve as an operational guide and general policy manual for The Berry Patch Bed & Breakfast.

Carol and Richard Jamm are looking to borrow $200,000 to purchase and reopen The Berry Patch Bed & Breakfast at Blueberry Hill in Canterbury, New Hampshire. $175,000 will go towards the purchase of the physical building and land, which consists of 2.5 acres. The remaining $25,000 will go towards upgrading the furnace, replace linens and dishes, and for initial marketing costs. The principals are also investing $50,000 of their own money; the extra $25,000 will allow them to invest all revenue into the business.

Table of Contents

Section One
The Business

Description of Business

The Berry Patch Bed & Breakfast is a rural five-room inn that caters to urban visitors, primarily from the Boston area. Room rates range from $85 to $125 a night. At the present time, annual occupancy rate is 60%.

The Nutts, the current owners, started The Berry Patch B&B in May, 1985. The business is open year-round and serves breakfast to overnight guests only.

The Berry Patch Bed & Breakfast is located in a heavily-trafficked tourist area, which means the occupancy rate is actually close to 100% during July and August. It drops off after Labor Day, but is booked solid on weekends in the late spring and early fall.

Occupancy can be increased year-round with special promotions and discounts during the off-season. Carol Jamm is a former marketing executive at Hilton Hotels, Inc., and is familiar with the kinds of marketing strategies that will attract guests to The Berry Patch Bed & Breakfast. She will also actively pursue local companies that need a small, private building for conferences and executive retreats

Description of the Market

The Berry Patch Bed & Breakfast will continue to provide restful nights in comfortable, antique-filled rooms to guests, along with a gourmet breakfast the next morning. We aim to increase the occupancy rate from 60% to 80% over the course of 18 months.

Our goal in operating The Berry Patch Bed & Breakfast is to

become a B&B that is known for its personalized service to guests, as well as our attention to detail. Our target market are young, unmarried couples in the Boston area, which is two hours south of The Berry Patch Bed & Breakfast.

We will pursue this desirable market with:

♦ Publicity in newspapers in Boston and throughout New England

♦ Advertising in Boston and New England lifestyle magazines

♦ Direct mail promotions to The Berry Patch's existing guest list

♦ Guest referral discounts on future stays

To pursue the corporate market we will:

♦ Make cold calls to travel plans at local and Boston corporations

♦ Invite qualified prospects for a free overnight stay

♦ Publicize and advertise the program in local and regional business publications

Description of Location

The Berry Patch Bed & Breakfast is located two miles outside of the village of Canterbury, on a quiet road with little traffic. This will appeal to guests who are looking for a quiet place to stay. Canterbury attracts many visitors who visit the Shaker village, which is the major tourist attraction in town. Concord, the state capitol, and the Lakes Region are a short drive away.

The house is a 13-room Cape built in 1803 with several additions made over the years. The guest rooms are quaint yet functional; the downstairs common areas are large and provide a quiet haven for guests. There is a broad expanse of lawn out back with a pond for swimming and ice skating. The land abuts a protected nature preserve where guests can wander on the hiking trails.

The owner's quarters consist of a two-bedroom apartment located in an ell off the back of the house.

Description of the Competition

There are two inns and one other B&B in Canterbury that will be competing directly with The Berry Patch Bed & Breakfast.

1) The Lincoln Bed & Breakfast is a three-room lodging facility located in the village of Canterbury. The rooms are not as luxurious as those at The Berry Patch Bed & Breakfast, and are priced at $50 a night per couple. The owner is a schoolteacher who runs the B&B as a sideline business. The Lincoln B&B is only open from May through October. She's been running the business for eight years and apparently has no plans to expand, since she has kept the B&B pretty much the same since she opened it.

2) The Shaker Inn is a 20-room inn located in an historic building. This inn also operates a full restaurant serving breakfast, lunch and dinner to the public as well as to guests.

A big part of the Inn's business focuses on weddings, banquets, and other private functions. Even though they have a large number of guest rooms, it almost seems as though the lodging business is operated almost as an afterthought.

Tourists who are not looking for the kind of intimacy that The Berry Patch Bed & Breakfast provides will prefer to stay at the Shaker Inn, if only they knew it existed, due to the lack of promotion.

The Inn has also experienced a change in management four times in five years, with new owners coming in twice during that period. We feel that this lack of stability contributes to the problems the Inn has had with both its identity and its occupancy rate.

3) The Lake House Bed & Breakfast is a four-room B&B that comes closest to what we hope to do with The Berry Patch Bed & Breakfast. The owners have operated the B&B for three years and do a lot of promotion and community-oriented events.

The Lake House Bed & Breakfast is elegant but not so sophisticated that it will scare some guests away. The Lake House's weak spot, however, is service, which we plan to stress at The Berry Patch Bed & Breakfast. Both of the principal owners at The Lake House work—one at an outside job, the other at a quilting business at home—and it seems like their attention is a bit scattered, because the B&B can be immaculate inside (we looked), but they can go a week without mowing the lawn. People notice things like that.

There are other inns and B&Bs in outlying towns along Route 112, but none offers the rural location that The Berry Patch Bed & Breakfast does.

Description of Management

Carol Jamm served as marketing manager for Hilton Hotels from 1987 through 1992, when she moved to New Hampshire with her husband specifically to look for a Country business to purchase and operate. She received an MBA in marketing from Boston University.

Her first jobs were with the Hilton Corporation, in the marketing departments at individual hotels in the chain.

Richard Jamm operated his own small construction business since graduating from high school. The size of his workforce has varied over the years, but he has managed at least five full-time employees at any one time.

Carol will be in charge of marketing and managing the office while Richard will handle the day-to-day operations as well as maintaining and making improvements to the physical plant.

The Jamms have retained the services of both an attorney and an accountant to help set up the business. They intend to join the local chamber of commerce, regional Country business association, and the tourism board in order to provide feedback and network with colleagues.

Description of Personnel

In the beginning, The Berry Patch Bed & Breakfast will hire one part-time employee to assist with serving breakfast, making up rooms, and general office work. He or she will be paid $5.50 an hour to start, with no benefits. We anticipate this job to consist of 20 hours a week. In slow times, this position will be cut down or out, depending on our slow season.

We don't anticipate the need for additional employees in the near future.

Application & Expected Effect of Loan or Investment

Purchase of Blueberry Hill property	$175,000
Renovations	25,000
Working capital	25,000
Cash reserve	<u>25,000</u>
Total:	$250,000

The Nutts, the current owners, are burned out of the business and are eager to sell, which helped to result in this favorable deal. Before our planned renovations, an independent appraisal company has assessed the property at $225,000.

Early renovations that we plan for the business include shoring up and reinforcing the sagging front porch, painting the exterior of the house, doing new landscaping, and generally sprucing up guest rooms and common areas where it's especially needed.

The amount of working capital will allow The Berry Patch Bed & Breakfast to pay the associated costs of transferring an existing business, joining trade associations, subscribing to industry newsletters, refurbishing inventory, meeting initial expenses, and building up a reserve fund for the off-season, when expenses remain constant but revenue dips drastically.

We've arranged with the Canterbury Bank for a special reserve line of credit to be used in case of major repairs to the house, or other emergencies. We will be investing $50,000 of our own funds towards the B&B.

Summary

The Berry Patch Bed & Breakfast is an elegant, low-key B&B where the emphasis is on service, a business concept that unfortunately seems to be in short supply. Carol and Richard Jamm, the prospective owners of The Berry Patch Bed & Breakfast, are seeking $200,000 to turn the business into what their vision of the ideal B&B should be. The money will enable them to set up the business, renovate and repair the property before reopening for business, have a line of credit in reserve along with adequate working capital in order to do the business right. This amount will allow the Jamms to bring the B&B through the transition from one owner to another, and to take the time necessary to convert The Berry Patch into a showplace.

There will always be a demand for lodging facilities in the Canterbury area. Even without doing anything, the previous owners were able to maintain a 60% occupancy rate with not a lot of effort. The combination of Carol's marketing savvy and Richard's entrepreneurial skills will ensure the increased and continued success of The Berry Patch Bed & Breakfast.

Section Two
Financial Data

Description of Sources and Applications of Funding

The Berry Patch Bed & Breakfast

Sources

1. Mortgage loan	$175,000
2. Line of credit	25,000
3. New investment from Jamms	50,000
Total:	$250,000

Applications

1. Purchase Blueberry Hill property	$175,000
2. Renovations	25,000
3. Working capital	25,000
4. Cash reserve for contingencies	25,000

To be secured by the assets of the business and personal guarantees of the principals, Carol and Richard Jamm.

Writing Your Marketing Plan

Though you do cover marketing to some extent in your business plan, developing and writing a separate, detailed marketing plan will serve the same clarifying purpose to your marketing efforts as to the development and daily operations of your country business.

Though you do have a lot of ideas to choose from in *Chapter Six: Marketing Your Country Business*, without a concrete plan to follow, it's easy to let marketing fall to the bottom of your daily and weekly to-do lists, or even fall off entirely.

Like a business plan, in your marketing plan you'll define your purpose as well as the target audience you wish to reach with the various tools in your marketing arsenal, you'll design a marketing budget that is reasonable and aggressive at the same time, pick your choice of media, along with the methods you'll use to evaluate their results. This will help you to alter your marketing plan for the following year.

For rural entrepreneurs who can't afford to hire a full-time marketing specialist, anything that involves promotional activity of any kind usually invites a shrug—or a sneer. After all, marketing is not most people's idea of a good time.

Marketing is usually considered to be an afterthought, something that is to be performed grudgingly when an advertising deadline looms or after you attend a trade association meeting and decide that your brochure and other promotional materials look painfully out of date compared to everyone else's.

One way to make marketing your business tolerable and even sometimes enjoyable is to map out a specific plan each year that won't let you off the hook so easily. If you say that in March it's time to send out your new brochure and start working on your newsletter, and that your budget that month allows for it, then you'll make sure that you do it.

The primary mistake that many rural entrepreneurs make in their marketing is to rely too heavily on advertising. I'm not saying that advertising doesn't work, because in some cases it can pull quite well. However, it often turns out to be the most expensive way to reach customers, especially when your one-inch display ad is only one of hundreds in a publication.

Advertising is easy, and also a known entity with a tangible product—but it doesn't necessarily produce the results you desire, which is an increase in the number of customers. Advertising is easy because you tell the sales rep what you want to say, you write out a check, go over the proof, and receive a copy of the magazine. In other words, somebody else does all the work. Spending your time and money on promotion—whether it's sending out a press kit or publicizing your web site—is harder, and doesn't provide you with a guaranteed entity, i.e., an ad in print, but what it will do is provide you with increased exposure among your targeted customers; they'll notice you simply because you'll stand out. After all, many rural entrepreneurs take the easy way out, spending the bulk of their annual marketing budget on advertising and perhaps printing another 1000 copies of their brochure with what's left over.

There are four different aspects to a marketing plan: The amount of time you will spend, on both a daily and weekly basis; the type of marketing you plan to do, from concentrating on magazine publicity, newspaper ads, or revamping your brochure and business cards; the amount of money you want to budget for each month and for the total year; and who's going to carry out each task—for some businesses, only one person will be responsible for writing copy, working with a graphic artist, and doing interviews with the press. Even for the smallest businesses, some business owners decide to spread out the responsibilities a) to insure they get done; and b) to provide a fresh eye. The type of customer you'd like to attract also enters into each of these aspects, broken down by region, profession, sex, income, and interests.

To draw up your annual marketing plan, you'll have to answer a lot of questions. You'll need to be as complete as possible, however, to design the best marketing plan for your business. By the way, marketing incorporates the following:

Advertising

Radio, newspaper, TV, magazines, and the Internet.

Direct Mail

Sending brochures to prospective and past customers, writing and editing a newsletter, sending information to other businesses that are in a position to refer customers to you.

Publicity

Sending letters, press releases and kits, making followup calls.

Other Areas

Planning special events, working with the chamber of commerce and other businesses.

Time

♦ How much time do you spend each week on marketing?

- Provide a breakdown of how many hours you'll spend each week on publicity, advertising, direct mail, and other areas. Do you feel this is enough time? Do you think you're using your time effectively?

- Would you like to spend more or less time? What would you spend it on, or where would you cut back?

- When are your busiest seasons? How far in advance should you begin planning for the various media and projects that you want to do?

- Look back over the last calendar year. Which months were slow in terms of business? Which were busy?

Media

- In which media would you like to focus more of your marketing efforts?

- What type of marketing brings you the most customers?

- What kind of customer would you like to see more of? How would you reach them?

Budget

- What percentage of total sales does your marketing budget comprise? How could you increase—or decrease—that amount? What other categories could you take money from?

- Do you have an annual or a monthly marketing budget now?

- Would you like to invest more money in one or more categories? Which ones? Why?

Execution

- Name the person or people currently responsible for marketing. Is there anyone else you feel comfortable assigning additional duties to?

- Are there additional tasks you could assign to a staff member that you don't like to do or don't have enough time for?

Customers

- In which area of the country do most of your customers live? Are they local or national?

- What type of customer would you like to see more of? How can you target them? Why would they be attracted to your business?

Think about your answers to these questions for a few days. Is there anything missing?

Sample Marketing Plan

Mary, the owner of the Dew Drop Inn, has been running the business for two years with Denise, her full-time assistant innkeeper. Most of her marketing budget has gone for advertising in regional magazines and ads in the weekly newspaper, and the annual guide the local tourism association publishes. Mary is unhappy with the results. Drawing up an annual marketing plan allowed her to revamp her strategy and anticipate certain times of the year that would require more time and money.

Her allotted budget of $3000 for the year—5% of gross revenue of $60,000—comes out to $250 a month. But the months that require more planning, and therefore more expenditures, are reflected in the chart.

To give you an idea of what a typical annual marketing plan looks like, here's one for a five-room country inn located in a rural area in northern New England.

Marketing Plan for the Dew Drop Inn

Goals

♦ To decrease reliance on advertising and create promotions that attract attention.

♦ To spread out marketing tasks between my full-time office assistant, Denise, and myself.

♦ To spend 10 hours a week on marketing.

♦ To bring in more families from the Boston area.

Keep in mind that this is how one country business does it. Use this format, but tailor your own marketing expectations and budget to the timetable.

Month	Media	Budget
January	**Direct Marketing** Denise Send discount weekend coupons to house list for March, when business tends to slow down.	Postage: $1000 \times .32 = \$320$ Stationery: $120 Printing coupon: $60
	Advertising Mary One weekly newspaper ad	$4 \times \$30 = \$120$

	Publicity Denise Send press release to local papers and magazines about March discount program	Postage: $10
February	**Direct Marketing** Mary Send brochures to prospective customers who call	Postage: 120 x .32 = $38.40
	Advertising Mary One weekly newspaper ad	4 x $30 = $120
March	**Advertising** Magazines send letters exhorting her to advertise in summer issues. Mary passes.	
	Publicity Mary Week of March 15th: Send and invitations to guidebook writers and newspaper travel editors in eastern Massachusetts for a press weekend in May. They also go to parenting magazines and writers in the Boston area.	$75 for postage & stationery

Also contact other area businesses that would like to cohost weekend.

April	**Direct Marketing** Denise Arrange to rent mailing list of tourists from chamber of commerce. Send letter & brochure for special family weekend in June.	$70 for list rental Postage: 700 x .32 = $224
	Publicity Mary Week of April 1st: Make followup calls to editors who received invitation for May weekend.	$40 (estimated)
May	**Publicity** Mary & Denise Weekend of 15th: Host press weekend	$300 for food & gas
June	**Direct Marketing** Denise For small convention business, go through local corporations, send a letter and brochure.	Postage & stationery: $100

July	**Advertising** Mary Weekly newspaper ad	4 x $30 = $120
	Publicity Denise Send press kit to national magazines about Christmas activities, with photos from last year.	$80
August	**Advertising** Mary Weekly newspaper ad	4 x $30 = $120
	Publicity Denise Followup calls from July	$40 phone bill (estimated)
September	**Advertising** Mary Weekly newspaper ad	4 x $30 = $120
	Take out ad in winter issue of regional magazine	$230
	Other Denise Start planning Christmas week activities with other businesses	

October	**Direct Marketing** Denise Letter to house list for Christmas week—special 5-day packages	500 x .32 = $160 Stationery: $60
	Other Denise Scour engagement announcements. Send brochure & wedding rates to the couples' parents and offer special discounts for guests	10 letters a week, $50 for one month
November	**Advertising** Mary Take out 1/6 page ad in regional tourism publication in spring	$230
December	**Advertising** Mary Weekly newspaper ad for Christmas activities	4 x $30 = $120
	Publicity Denise Call editors to confirm if they'll attend Christmas week activities	$40 (estimated)
		Grand Total: **$2967.40**

Starting a Country Business From Scratch

If you decide to start your country business from scratch, you will need to do more work from the beginning than if you bought an existing country business. The advantage is that it costs less; the downside is that it will take more time before you open it.

There's also a lot more detail and legal work to do if you start from scratch, which includes getting a business license, meeting local health and fire codes, and setting yourself up as a business, all of which is covered in *Chapter Four: Country Business Start-Up*

The main disadvantage to starting a country business from scratch is that you won't have income from the business until you open your doors, and possibly not for a few months after that. In fact, while you do pay more at the outset for an existing country business, it can start producing revenue for you from the day you move in. In fact, many rural entrepreneurs who started from scratch say that if they had it to do over again, that they would buy an existing country business. You should weigh the pros and cons against your own temperament before you proceed.

If you do decide to buy an existing country business, most of it has already been set up for you, from the zoning approvals to the insurance, though you do have to change everything over into your name.

Buy An Existing Country Business

Buying a country business means that you have the advantage of a hopefully good reputation, and an established list of customers who are familiar with your country business. In addition, people may already be familiar with your country business, even if they haven't been customers in the past; this gives you another pool of potential customers to pursue.

Sometimes, buying an existing country business will actually cost less than starting from scratch if you factor in the customer list, equipment, and the reputation of the business; all of these are included in the purchase price. And if you figure that your labor is worth something, even though you probably won't be paying yourself a salary for quite some time, buying a country business outright may turn out to be a veritable bargain.

Does Buying An Existing Rural Business Equal Buying A Job?

According to John Stimets, a business broker selling New England businesses for Country Business, Inc., in Burlington, Vermont, one of the quickest ways to gain acceptance into a rural community is to purchase a local business.

You may still be viewed as the outsider for a while, but the acceptance period is considerably shortened. The ownership of a business carries with it a certain stature within the community. You have immediate impact because you are employing others who can be helpful in introducing you to others and familiarizing you with the area.

The fact that you are controlling economic dynamics (suppliers, customers, banking, professionals, employees, service providers, etc.) will in itself serve your immediate needs of fitting into the community.

Buying any business is a major undertaking, but buying a rural business will require additional foresight and due diligence. The size and type of business must be weighed against your skills, finances, interests and goals.

Owning a business will generally require a greater commitment than seeking employment. Once you buy a business, it will not be easy to reverse that decision if it doesn't work out. Remember that not all prospective entrepreneurs will share your dream of being in the sticks. It must be something you are comfortable working at daily and not just a reason to move to a certain community.

In considering a small business, you must determine if it is a "buy a job" type of business or one with upside potential. One will have reasonable parameters established as to time and financial commitment while the other will only be bound by your managerial and financial limitations. Both will most likely consume most of your time initially leaving you with little to worry about free-time activities. Eventually, those free-time activities will be available, but by then you will be an integral part of the town, able to choose your leisure time agenda.

There are additional considerations that should be part of the decision-making process when investigating a rural business. For instance, will the mayor or another influential person in the town be one of your employees? Do your customers come to the business because of its location or niche or do they patronize it because of the exiting owner? Are you or your spouse going to replace a popular "townie" once you acquire the business? This line of questioning will be instrumental in your long-term success in a small community.

Like all decisions of moving to the country, buying a business will require careful planning. it is generally recommended that you choose a particular type of businesses within a fairly broad geography rather than narrowing our choices by stating that you want to own a business in a particular community and then trying to pigeonhole into it. This could start you into the process with blinders on.

Patience will be the key if this is an alternative you are seeking. Recognizing the type of business you want should be the driving force behind your decision. The rest will fall into place.

Country Business Profile
Furniture Maker

John Alden
Gorham, Maine

Description of Business

Making chairs, tables and other items for individuals and retail stores.

Ease of Startup

Moderate. Many woodworkers have had shops set up for years.

Range of Initial Investment

$3,000-5,000 for equipment and supplies.

Time Commitment

Part-or full-time

Can You Run the Business From Home?

Yes

Success Potential

Moderate. There's a lot of competition out there. If you specialize in one area and are skilled, your chances are good.

How to Market the Business

Advertising, word of mouth, referrals, through retail furniture shops.

The Pros

If you've always worked with wood as a hobby, doing it for money will be a joy.

The Cons

It takes time to build up a clientele. You might have to charge a lot to make money or cut your prices to sell your work.

Special Considerations

Custom and hand-built furniture is in demand, though it can be affected by the economy and a limited market.

For More Information

Fine Woodworking Magazine, POB 5506, Newtown, CT 06470.

Story of the Business

With traditional Yankee foresight and caution, John Alden, who builds furniture with an emphasis on Early American styles, planned his retirement business according to a blueprint that would work for many aspiring entrepreneurs. He began planning his business a few years before he retired, developing it while still working at his job as engineer. He retired at age 62 to work full-time building furniture, taking time for a little sailing, now and then.

Alden has always built furniture. During the Depression he and his family made most of their own furniture. When he had children of his own, he made a lot of his family's furniture. "I enjoyed it and thought I would start doing it for other people," he explains. "While I was working at my job, I began to get things ready so when I retired I could start right in."

In the beginning Alden advertised in local papers and distributed a brochure to attract customers. After he developed a reputation in the area, he discontinued the brochure and ads. He says that if he continued the marketing, he'd get more business than he could handle by himself. He has no desire to add to his business by having employees. "I keep busy just by word of mouth," he indicates.

John made chairs and other items for a furniture shop in Connecticut, but he says there were problems. "When you build furniture by hand, it's difficult to make it inexpensively enough so a shop can double the price and still have it be affordable," he explains. "I prefer to sell direct. That way I can price pieces so they're reasonable enough that people can afford them."

To determine the price of a chair, Alden accounts for his overhead, estimates the cost of the materials he uses and adds in the labor he puts into a piece. He's built clocks, chests of drawers and tables.

Windsor chairs are the most labor-intensive piece he builds, taking 20 hours for each chair. He prices a side chair at $350 and an armchair at $450.

Alden gets most of his wood from his 50 acres of woodland. "I try to use the same species of wood that would have been used in the original," he points out. "I cut and dry the timber here in my own building and use it as airdried lumber."

He works 50 hours a week, which is more than he spent at his engineer position, but says he thoroughly enjoys it. "I work a full day nearly every day, but I don't feel pressured to do it," he says.

"My goals are quite different from someone who's starting a new business because I have no desire to build it up and have employees," he remarks. "Consequently I end up doing many of the menial tasks that would normally get passed on to an employee, like cleaning and getting rid of the sawdust."

Though he specializes in chairs, he does do custom work, building whatever a customer wants. "My expertise is the ability to copy Early American pieces," he says.

"I'm going to stick with it as long as I'm physically able. This kind of work gives me the opportunity so that when the weather is right for sailing, I sail. The other days I work in the shop. And people understand."

Country Business Profile
Nursery

Alpine Gardens
Ron Backhaus
Bethel, Vermont

Description of Business

A specialized nursery that sells trees and contracts custom landscape work.

Ease of Startup

Moderate. You order the plants, set them out and wait.

Range of Initial Investment

$1,000 and up for trees and plants.

Time Commitment

Part-or full-time

Can You Run the Business From Home?

Yes

Success Potential

Moderate. Demand for a specialized nursery stock is less than for conventional nursery stock. It can take years before trees are mature and ready to sell.

How to Market the Business

Advertising, word of mouth, referrals.

The Pros

You can time things so that you start the nursery before you retire; then when you've left your job, the trees will be ready to sell.

The Cons

It takes time to build up a clientele, especially with unusual kinds of plants and trees.

Special Considerations

A nursery will work for people who love to dig in the dirt and don't need immediate income.

Story of the Business

Ron Backhaus has an unusual nursery in an area that's not noted for its delicate plant life. Alpine Gardens specializes in dwarf conifers, small varieties bred from needle-leaf trees like pine or spruce. Ron became interested in dwarf conifers at his previous home in Long Island, where a neighbor grew and sold them.

"I liked their style and the life that goes with it," he explains. "It's not like perennials where you have to cut them down every year."

When he moved to Vermont in 1985 Ron supplemented his retirement income by mowing lawns until the business got established. Like a winery, the trees need time to mature. Dwarf conifers can take a lot longer than many wines to mature: Some varieties take from five to seven years.

He set aside three of his 10 acres for the nursery. There are about 1,000 trees planted at any one time. Now that there are a number of mature trees to sell, he plants new trees every year to replace the ones bought by customers.

In spring Backhaus cleans up the gardens that have been damaged by winter and fertilizes the soil. In May and June, the cuttings he ordered over the winter arrive and are put into the ground. People come to buy trees for their gardens, or sometimes they contract Backhaus to design and plant a dwarf conifer garden for them.

In the summer, people have done their buying until fall, but Ron has to weed and mulch the garden. In September and early fall, he plants again to replace the trees he's sold. In October he starts to prepare the nursery for winter, which he sees as his time off. "Catalogs come in by the millions then. If I want cuttings for spring delivery, I order them in December," he says.

Spring and fall, Ron spends six hours a day, seven days a week outside working in the nursery and planting clients' gardens. "It's a long day, and it's not easy work," he says. "You have to do lots of cultivating, you have to weed, and the weather can be a problem. I want to make my nursery a showpiece, so I put in my own dwarf conifer gardens as a display."

Backhaus has done some local advertising in weekly papers. A couple of articles in local papers have boosted his business. "I don't have large quantities of trees. My trees are relatively more expensive because it takes so long for them to become a salable item," he says. His trees sell from $25 to $150, depending on their age.

He wants to keep the nursery as a small and manageable business. "A specialized nursery is good for me because I'm not interested in getting much bigger," he remarks. "This is a very selective, small market. If I were younger, I think I'd be more diversified and have other plants to sell that are compatible with dwarf conifers."

Since dwarf conifers are not well known, Backhaus's biggest problem is teaching people what dwarf conifers are. "Most people are used to doing a lot of fertilizing. Dwarf conifers just don't need it," he says. "Some people think dwarf conifers are just plants that haven't grown up yet."

Chapter Four

Country Business Start-Up

All the factors and details involved in starting a business usually serve as the proving ground of a business:

After all, if you're still enthusiastic about running a country business after you've gotten through all the grunt work of everything that's necessary to get a business up and running, then you know you've made the right decision.

Even if you've fallen a bit out of love with your country business after the startup tasks, you shouldn't worry, because the moment you start to work with your first customer, all the reasons why you wanted to start a country business in the first place will come rushing back at you.

You just have to jump through a few hoops first.

Your Country Business & The Law

With any business, there are certain legal restrictions that you have to meet in order to do business. The first thing you need to do is register your business with the state. There will be a fee for this, and the purpose is to make sure no other business is currently operating with your name. If there is, you will have to find another name for your country business.

Registration will also alert the state to expect tax revenue from your business. If you don't file a return with the state, they'll know where to find you.

When you register with the state, you should also ask about other regulations you have to meet in order to operate your particular type of business in your state. Most of the time, they will refer you to your town itself, which is responsible for determining zoning and other business regulations, since it will collect the fees from any permits for renovations that you will need to do.

I will get into the nitty gritty of the various bureaucracies later in this chapter. The important things at this point is to find out what departments the state, town, or county are each responsible for, the type of registration you will have to make with each, and to make sure you comply with all of them. If you neglect any one of the steps necessary to open and operate a country business in your town, the government authorities at any level have the power necessary to shut down your business and/or do whatever is necessary in order to bring your business up to code. The time to find all of this out is before you open your doors. This is important even if you're buying an existing business, since the codes may have changed since the owners started their business, and certain aspects may have been grandfathered in, and the clause may expire when a new owner assumes ownership. Or else, the town fathers have just looked the other way because the owners were friends or family, but they're going to come down hard on you, especially if you're a newcomer to town. If they catch you later because you neglected something because you didn't know about it, you won't be able to use your ignorance as an excuse. So it pays to do your homework first.

You also need to think about the form your business will take: a sole proprietorship, partnership, or a corporation. Each has its advantages and disadvantages, and rural entrepreneurs have very specific reasons for picking one over the others.

Sole Proprietorship

A sole proprietorship is the form of business that most single-owner businesses pick. It's easy to start—all you have to do is register with the state and you're in business—you make all the decisions yourself, and besides zoning and other regulations connected with running a country business, you're pretty much free from having to follow complex laws regarding the operation of your business. You alone are responsible for the success or failure of your business, and any profits your business earns are reported as income in your name.

However, because there are few restrictions on a sole proprietorship when you run into legal or financial trouble, it falls on your shoulders to deal with it. For instance, if a client slips and falls on the front steps at your place of business, he can sue you personally; any savings or investments you have—including your equity in the business itself—is fair game for the client and a hungry lawyer who sees your house as a piggy bank that needs to be shaken.

For many country businesses, liability insurance that's tied in with your business or homeowners policy will often be enough to handle a "reasonable" lawsuit and settlement. The remote chances of being hit with a lawsuit and the relative ease of operating this form of business ownership make a sole proprietorship the preferred method of business organization for most rural entrepreneurs.

However, if your business should fail, you will be responsible for all outstanding debts incurred during the course of doing business. If you don't pay them, or declare bankruptcy, it will be reflected on your personal credit record.

Partnerships

A partnership is actually two sole proprietorships combined. This means that while the strengths are doubled, so are the inherent weaknesses.

A rural entrepreneur will frequently decide to create a partnership when they enter the business with a friend or business partner. Married couples sometimes decide to form a partnership for their country business. Though a partnership means more energy and money than a sole proprietorship because more than one person is involved, a partnership should be entered into with extreme caution.

The best partnerships work when the partners have differing but complementary talents—and they leave the other partner alone to do what he does best. For instance, at one country business, one partner may have a background in marketing while the other will be responsible for the day-to-day business operations. As long as each trusts the other to concentrate on her own department, and to interfere only when problems arise, then the partnership will probably do well.

Partnerships usually run into trouble when the partners have similar skills and/or different ideas about the right way to run a business. For example, when both partners want to maintain all the contact with clients, but not deal with bookkeeping or sending out overdue invoices, there are going to be problems right from the start.

Like a sole proprietorship, if a client decides to sue, both partners are personally liable. And if the business fails leaving outstanding debts, again, you are both responsible. You should also be aware that if one partner disappears after the failure of a country business, the other must pay all debts. Be aware of this, because this does happen from time to time.

Corporations

A corporation is best defined as an inanimate object, a business organization that has its own needs aside from those of the business, which include financial and legal restrictions. It's more difficult, expensive and time-consuming to form and then operate your country business as a corporation, but it also absolves your formal personal responsibility in case business sours or a customer or supplier decides to sue.

One advantage that corporations have over partnerships or sole proprietorships is that they can raise money by selling shares in the business; the only recourse the other two have is to borrow money from a bank or from friends.

But a corporation is by nature more unwieldy than the other two because of its responsibility to its shareholders, who are really part-owners. The IRS taxes corporations on a different scale from sole proprietorships and partnerships, and there are even more rules and regulations a corporation must follow on both the state and federal level.

There are also certain restrictions on the types of operations a corporation can run—some expansion and growth issues, for example, require the approval of stockholders before a project can proceed.

Some rural entrepreneurs automatically opt for incorporation to protect personal assets, but the kind of country business that will benefit most from incorporation is when there are more than two owners; issues of ownership and decision-making become more complex with that many owners, so it makes it easier to rely on a board of directors and group of stockholders, especially since they've invested their money and trust in the business.

Do You Need An Attorney?

Whether or not you choose to use the services of an attorney to help you start your country business depends on how you view the legal profession and how detail-oriented you are. Some rural entrepreneurs swear by their lawyers and consult with them about every decision that needs to be made. Others swear at them, and will never use an attorney for anything in their business or personal lives.

The happy medium is somewhere in between. If you're planning to incorporate your country business, you'll probably need to use a lawyer, although more people are learning how to incorporate themselves. I feel that the vast majority use a lawyer to help facilitate the process.

If you're buying a country business or a house to use for your country business, you will undoubtedly have to hire an attorney to do a title search and to help prepare a warranty deed for the property. But aside from these tasks, you will probably be able to do most of the tasks involved in starting your country business without a lawyer.

Do You Need An Accountant?

If you're unsure about the type of business organization that suits you best—sole proprietorship, partnership, or corporation—it's a good idea to consult with an accountant to help you decide, who will analyze your current financial situation and help you determine what you want to gain from the country business—equity or income—and advise you about how to best achieve your goals.

An accountant can also analyze the books and financial records of a country business you're considering purchasing. It's a good idea to find an accountant who has some experience working with your particular industry; ask other similar businesses in the area for the names of their accountants. Then call them up and interview them before you settle on one.

An accountant can also help you set up a realistic budget and a schedule of projected revenues. And if this is the first time you've run a business of your own, she can also help you become familiar with different accounting methods and the tax rates based on projected revenue and the tax codes of your state. She can also recommend methods of bookkeeping that will make her job that much easier when tax season rolls around.

Insurance & Bonds

The first thing you should do is to check with your own insurance agency to see if your policy has provisions for extra coverage for your customers. If all they offer is a commercial policy that offers more coverage than you actually need, shop around for another agency that will give you what you want without overinsuring you.

There are several kinds of insurance that you should carry. You should first check your current homeowners' policy, because some companies prohibit their clients from operating any kind of venture on the insured premises.

Be prepared for the shock of paying two to five times the premium that you're paying now.

Though liability insurance is the most important kind for you to carry, you'll probably also need to have coverage for theft, fire and water damage.

If you can arrange for one insurance company to cover all of these different kinds of insurance for you, you'll probably pay less than you would if you spread the policies among a number of different agencies. The premium you'll pay will also be affected by the deductible you choose, and can vary from a few hundred dollars up to $10,000 or more.

Licenses & Permits

Before you spend one penny on renovations or improvements to your country business, you must check with the local, county and state business authorities to find out about the various kinds of licenses and permits you'll need and the fire and health codes you'll need to meet in order to be licensed as a business.

These vary from town to town and from state to state, so I'm not going to go into detail about them here.

I will, however, describe the purpose of the licenses and permits you will be required to get. Bear in mind, however, the stringency of these requirements will also vary as well. States and regions with more highly regulated governments tend to be pickier about the quality of your country business.

Even though you may resent all the legalese and paperwork, it's important to meet all of the requirements. No one says you can't complain every step of the way, however.

- You'll need a sales tax certificate from the state to collect tax.

- You'll probably need to have the local fire inspector check for properly marked fire exits, smoke alarms in each room and in common areas, and to check if your house is adequately constructed and protected against fire. In some cases, an older building would pass fire code, but if the owners planned to renovate or if you build an entirely new building, the code is more stringent and may include the construction of special firewalls designed to restrict the spread of fire as well as custom fire escapes that can be accessed from each room. Hard-wired smoke and fire detectors are a must in most new construction or renovations, as well. Some fire codes may even require expensive sprinkler systems to be built, along with a fire alarm system.

- Depending upon the business, a health inspector will ascertain whether your septic and water systems can accommodate the demands that an increase in visitors will place on them.

- Even if your home and facilities successfully meet all of the above regulations, if your home is not in an area that is zoned for business use, you may be out of luck.

Your town government determines zoning and is also responsible for making exceptions for businesses that are located outside of commercial zones. Though your country business will provide a tax base for your town, since it is a commercial enterprise operating (most likely) in a residential area, you will probably have to apply for a zoning variance.

The rules get creative, though. Some towns will allow you to operate as a country business in a residential area as long as you don't put a sign out. Others will require that you as owner live in the house and not in a separate building. You may also have to expand your driveway and parking area to accommodate an increased number of cars.

And far more interesting laws governing country businesses undoubtedly exist. That's why it's important to check all of the requirements *before* you do anything.

Country Business Profile
Cat Kennel

The Cat's Pajamas
Toni Miele
Lincolnville, Maine

Description of Business

A luxury boarding facility geared toward cats and kittens who stay overnight or longer.

Ease of Startup

Difficult. You need to build a separate, heated facility that has the cats' best interests at heart.

Range of Initial Investment

At least $20,000 to build the facility.

Time Commitment

Full-time

Can You Run the Business From Home?

Yes

Success Potential

Easy. Yet another niche that combines quality with caring, important factors when it comes to people and their pets.

How to Market the Business

Newspaper advertising, publicity, word of mouth and repeat business.

The Pros

It's perfect for cat lovers.

The Cons

You can't leave spontaneously; you must arrange for backup care.

Special Considerations

Many kennels have all the charm of a barracks. With a homey focus on cats, this business will receive a lot of attention, and therefore, business.

For More Information

American Boarding Kennels Association, 4575 Galley Rd. #400A, Colorado Springs, CO 80915

Story of the Business

As with many entrepreneurs, Toni Miele started her business when she couldn't find a particular service she needed. "In 1987, my husband Michael and I went overseas for six months," she recalls. "The only problem we had was finding a quality boarding facility for our three cats. When we got back, I decided to open my own. When we designed and built our own house, we planned the cat kennel as part of the house. The cats are on the ground floor, and we're on the top floor."

Toni worked as a respiratory therapist for many years. In opening the kennel, she started working at what she always wanted to do as a child: taking care of animals.

There are no cages. The cats' space is L-shaped with commercial grade linoleum. There are upper and lower sleeping lofts in each of the cats' "rooms." Every cat gets a sheepskin to lie on, and there's a floor-to-ceiling climbing pole made of sisal rope. The rooms are eight feet tall and designed for two cats, with 72 cubic feet per cat. Michael, who's a builder, helped with the construction, which kept the costs down.

"They can get a lot of exercise in the room, but I allow each cat out into the room, one at a time, all day long," says Toni. "They play in an exercise area with a cat tree and a car

"You want to be very different from what the competition is doing so people can make an intelligent selection. I'm different because of the amount of space for each cat, the excellence of service and the degree of care," she continues. The Cat's Pajamas is one of the few kennels in the area that can accommodate multi-cat families and long-term boarding.

Miele's business grosses about $50,000 each year, and her operating expenses are low. "Food and litter go up," she points out, "but you get smarter about ordering and usage."

Miele says this is the best business she could ever be in. "I'm doing something I would be doing anyway. I have lots of free time, and I don't have to commute or dress up. During my lunch break, I can go out and bicycle or kayak on the bay."

The only members of the Miele household who might not be enthusiastic are her three cats, who never venture into the kennel.

Country Business Profile
Winery

Chateau Chevre
Jerry Hazen
Yountville, California

Description of Business

A vineyard that sells grapes whole-sale and makes its own wine on the premises.

Ease of Startup

Difficult. It's expensive, requires permits and takes four to five years to develop the grapes; it takes another one or two to make the wine.

Range of Initial Investment

At least $500,000 for the land and expenses.

Time Commitment

Part-time while you develop the vineyard; full-time when you start making wine.

Can You Run the Business From Home?

Yes

Success Potential

Difficult. Competition, poor weather and economy as well as the reduced drinking habits of Americans has made this business difficult in recent years.

How to Market the Business

Through publicity to travel and wine writers, advertising to tourists, holding wine tastings.

The Pros

If you like wine, you'll feel like a baron once you're up and running.

The Cons

It's expensive, takes a lot of hard work, and there are no guarantees. To a great extent, you're totally dependent on the weather.

Special Considerations

Land in California's Napa Valley is pricey. Small vineyards in out-of-the-way places like Idaho, Washington state and Vermont have a better chance.

For More Information

American Wine Society, 3006 Latta Road, Rochester, NY 14612.

Story of the Business

In 1972 Jerry Hazen was an airline pilot, 50 years old, and starting to think about what he would do when he retired in eight more years. He bought 12 acres in the Napa Valley that was little more than pastureland, with the idea of planting grapes on it.

In 1973 he started to put in the vineyard because he knew it would take at least four years for the first crop of quality grapes to come forth. Though his initial plan was to just sell the grapes, he made a batch of homemade wine from the first crop in 1977.

He entered it in some wine tastings where it won blue ribbons. The judges suggested he make wine as well as sell grapes. By the time he was able to sell the first crop of grapes in 1978, Hazen had caught the wine bug.

He spent 18 months applying for the permits necessary to make wine in the Napa Valley. This involved separate inspections by the state and county governments.

They checked to see that the property had adequate water, since winemaking uses a lot of water. They considered whether the land was near any earthquake lines, and they wanted to know how he would dispose of waste materials. By the end of 1979, after he'd been through all this, he discovered he could have received a verbal permit to sell the wine in 1978. He had already sold all of that year's crop, so he officially began in 1979.

He named his winery *Chateau Chevre*, because the 1,300-square-foot building that was converted into the winery once served as a barn for goats; Chateau Chevre is French for goat house.

Hazen produces both red and white wines. He ages them in French oak barrels, which are supposed to be the best. Some wineries are using oak from the Northwest, and he says it's hard to tell the difference.

He ages his table red wine in the barrels for 22 months; his

Merlot takes about three years. Hazen also makes Chardonnay, which takes about a year to age. He doesn't grow Chardonnay grapes; instead he buys the grapes from a friend down the road.

Hazen bottles the wine by hand, using semiautomatic corking machines. He and a team of friends can bottle 350-400 cases in a day. Chateau Chevre's annual output is about 1,000 cases a year, down from 5,000 in 1987, when he had a partner who thought bigger was better. Hazen didn't agree; they parted ways. Today, he feels that 1,000 cases annually is manageable.

Fall is the busiest season at the winery because the grapes are picked and crushed. "You have to pick the grapes when the sugar's at a certain level. If you pick them a little late in the season, you lose some of the texture of the wine," explains Jerry. He says that the optimal sugar content produces a wine with an alcohol content of 13 to 13-1/2 percent.

"The grapes are what set me apart from everyone else," he remarks. "Merlot is a very popular grape. You can't do much to influence the quality of your grapes, however. You should get good grapes to start with and take care of them. Then do a bit of adjusting in the laboratory, and let nature take care of the rest."

Early reaction to Hazen's wine was positive, so he didn't have to do much in the way of marketing. "They came to me," he recalls, referring to wine brokers and distributors.

Chateau Chevre also received favorable ratings in the publications *The Wine Spectator*, *Wine Advocate* and *Connoisseur's Guide to Wine*. People would read about the wine; they either called the winery directly or asked their local liquor store to order it. Hazen's brokers also visit liquor stores and restaurants to sell the wine.

He lists the winery in local guide maps and trade papers. There are a fair number of tourists who visit the winery by appointment and buy directly from Hazen.

Business has dropped in the last few years. Hazen, setting his price by the supply and demand, has dropped a couple of dollars off the price of each bottle. He doesn't feel that the fact that people are drinking less is responsible; he believes lack of easy money is the problem. "I still sell the wine, but more slowly," he reports. A bottle of Merlot goes for $14, and Chardonnay costs $12. Hazen grosses about $70,000 each year, with grape sales accounting for about 40 percent of that.

Country Business Profile
Photographer

Photographs by Dike Mason
Dike Mason
Wiscasset, Maine

Description of Business

A professional photographer shoots special events and everyday subjects as well.

Ease of Startup

Easy. You need skill and some adequate equipment.

Range of Initial Investment

$5,000.

Time Commitment

Part- or full-time

Can You Run the Business From Home?

Yes

Success Potential

Moderate. If you limit your work to specific kinds of photography while you're building a business, you will limit the number of jobs. Later on, it helps to specialize.

How to Market the Business

Advertising, publicity, word of mouth, referrals.

The Pros

If you've always been a hobbyist, it's very satisfying to make a living from photography.

The Cons

It's very competitive; there are a lot of amateur photographers who call themselves professionals.

Special Considerations

You have to be as tireless in running your business as your are pursuing great photos. If you don't want to promote yourself, it'll be hard to succeed.

For More Information

Professional Photographers of America, 1090 Executive Way, Des Plaines, IL 60018.

Story of the Business

"I'm really an entrepreneur pursuing my hobby, and I get other people to pay for it," reveals Dike Mason, a professional photographer who had dabbled in photography during his professional career as a mechanical engineer at General Electric and an officer in the military. "Some people say, 'What a great photograph!' and write out a check. Others say, 'What a great photograph!' and don't want to pay for it. The truth is I do better quality work if I'm getting paid, because if someone's paying me I try to do the best job I can."

Mason has been carrying a camera with him since the 1930s, when he spent a vacation hiking the Appalachian Trail. "I started taking photos of children, and I've been doing it ever since," he recalls.

Dike's work has been displayed in shows organized by the Photographic Society of America. He doesn't shoot for weddings or graduations except for relatives. He focuses on theatrical photography for local dramatic groups, which he says is dramatic, fun and requires a few technical tricks. "I work at dress rehearsals; I shoot three or four rolls of film, take the best six and blow them up to put in the lobby," he says. "The cast loves to have their photos, and I make extra prints for them." He does his own developing at home.

Most of the groups are local nonprofit repertory companies. He rarely charges for his time, only for materials. But since many of the actors order extra prints, Mason can make up to $200 from one shoot.

To get other work, he runs a small, one-inch display ad in a local weekly paper, the *Maine Times*. The ad reads: "Photographs by Dike Mason. Practice limited to subjects of interest." It then lists his phone number. "I get a lot of calls from that ad because so many people see it," he says. "I took out the ad because a friend who's also a freelance photographer told me that if you're going to take up photography, you must have a local ad appear regularly. That way you can get professional prices without a fight."

The ad provides him with instant credibility, which has been its biggest utility. The rest of his business is generated through word of mouth.

He says advertising also brands you as a professional in the darkroom. Without that distinction, people are always comparing your prices to the 35-cent print they can get at the drugstore. "The small prints will kill you," he says, referring to 3 x 5 and 5 x 7 prints. "An 8 x 10 isn't any more work than a 5 x 7, but you make twice as much money, and the increased cost of materials is negligible."

Mason says that if you're going to go into the business seriously, quality equipment is essential. "You need at least a couple of cameras and some darkroom equipment to get started," he reports. "I started with used equipment and have used it for a good part of my life. I've also been able to get some new equipment; that's the good thing about making some money from photography." Three or four cameras and a dozen lenses add up pretty fast, though he says a professional photographer doesn't need this kind of equipment to start out.

"I think of my camera as expendable," he remarks. "They do wear out. I spend a lot of time sailing in the salt air with them." Work is pretty steady throughout the year, though sometimes a few weeks will go by without any jobs. Then all of a sudden, five jobs will come in that all need to be done at once.

Mason also does some video work, mostly for local cable channels and documentaries. He says the work is fascinating, but that it's difficult to make any money from it.

"Video's hard, because it's difficult to get people to pay for considerably better quality," he indicates. "They feel they can do it themselves for free, even thought they don't do a great job. I don't see a great future in it.

"I carry my camera everywhere I go," he says. "It makes me look at things I never would have thought of looking at. They come out of the blue, and when they come, I'm available for them."

Chapter Five

Operating Your Country Business

Operations—the day-to-day routine you set up and follow in order to maintain some semblance of organization in your country business—is not the most fun or creative parts of your business. In fact, it can be downright boring. But neglecting these steps and running your daily operations in a haphazard way is the quickest way to drive your country business into the ground. Take some time now to set daily operations policy; later on, it will mean that you'll have more time and attention to pay to the fun stuff.

Estimating Operating Costs

Every business has its cycles when business is booming and then when it stops dead in its tracks.

Some businesses can experience ups and downs that can swing radically several times a year. The bad news is that some expenses—like the mortgage and utilities—remain constant.

If you are purchasing an existing country business, estimating your operating costs will be easy. Just ask the current owners for a full year's breakdown of expenses along with the current income statement. If possible, go through the expenses with the owners asking about the budgeted amounts and the actual expenses. If you are starting from scratch, it will be a little more difficult.

Aside from sheer guesswork, the best way to estimate your operating costs is to contact the suppliers you'll be dealing with. They will probably be very helpful.

Following is a chart that contains all possible expenses you may encounter in running a country business. I won't provide estimates, since they can vary so widely depending on the type of business you're running, how ambitious your plans are, the area of the country you live in, and how extravagant you make your office, among other things.

It's a good idea to chart the expenses for each month for a year. Some are optional, and you can cut down on some expenses you can do yourself.

The House

Mortgage
Taxes
Insurance
Utilities
Heat

Office Expenses

Telephone
Separate fax line
Credit card commissions
Postage

Stationery supplies

Printing
Advertising
Trade association dues & memberships
Accountant & attorney fees
Contract employees, freelancers or consultant expenses

Company Vehicle

Loan
Registration
Insurance
Gas

Employee Expenses

Payroll
Taxes
Insurance
Workers' compensation
Bonuses
Discounts

Capital Improvements

Furniture upgrades
Computer equipment upgrades
Electronic equipment upgrades

Keeping Good Records

It's important to keep track of your expenses and revenue sources. On the one hand, it will make things easier for you at tax time, but it's also enlightening to know how much you spent in every category last year, and to figure out how much money you could save at the end of the year by streamlining it in some way.

There are as many ways to keep records as there are rural entrepreneurs. Some rely on one of several computer programs especially designed for small businesses, while some stuff receipts in shoeboxes and dump them out and add them up at the end of the year.

No matter which method you choose, make it easy to do and organize it so you can do it immediately instead of saving up the work to be done in one lump at the end of the week. If you're like most rural entrepreneurs, you won't be able to find a block of time anywhere in your week unless it's in the middle of the night.

And in the unlikely case of a tax audit somewhere down the road, it will help your case if you can show the auditor receipts that provide answers to all of his questions. Keeping good records will also help facilitate figuring out the deductions you'll be able to take.

Keeping good records also helps you determine your monthly and annual sales figures, as well as knowing where each customer heard about you. When planning future marketing campaigns, you'll know which ad or promotion brought in the most customers.

But keeping adequate records just makes good common sense. At the very least, get a ledger book. Some business checking accounts now offer a built-in ledger that allows you to break down the checks you write into different expense categories eliminating the need for a separate ledger.

Accounting Basics

In running your country business, you need to keep track of revenue coming in and expenses going out. It's a good idea to set up an accounting system that works best for you and your business.

There are two kinds of accounting you can use to track revenue and expenses. One, cash accounting, involves simple bookkeeping where income is recorded when it is received, and expenses that are paid are recorded when bills go out, even if the expense was incurred in a different month. With cash accounting, you will record the revenue in the month where it may not have necessarily occurred, which may give you an inaccurate picture of your business cycles if you rely on revenue alone to show the health of your business, and not month-to-month occupancy rate. Cash accounting, however, is a very simple way to keep your books, and rural entrepreneurs who have several income-generating vocations, which is a common occurrence, prefer it for its simplicity. They don't need a precise picture of their month to month revenue and expense picture.

Accrual accounting is more painstaking in its execution, but it gives a more accurate view of revenue and expenses, and of your monthly financial situation. Even though payment may be received or credited the following month—and expenses paid on a net 30 system since the expenses occurred in the previous month, they are recorded in that month's ledgers, and not when they were actually paid.

When drawing up your accounting sheets, no matter which method you choose, refer to the categories named in the previous section, *Estimating Operating Costs*. You may want to list certain expenses in categories that are even more specific. Again, bear in mind the method and categories that will work best for your country business.

Hiring Employees

Some rural entrepreneurs prefer to keep their operations small, specifically so they'll be able to handle all the jobs themselves without having to hire outside help. Hiring and managing employees adds a whole new dimension into your business and has both its good and bad points: For one, it means more paperwork because you'll have to pay state, federal, and perhaps local payroll taxes in addition to Social Security and workmen's compensation, and health insurance—that is, if you decide to offer it. On the other hand, having someone around to help out with the grunt work means you'll have more time to focus on running and building your business, like marketing your country business

But unfortunately, a common complaint of business owners everywhere today is that it's hard to find good help; after all, no paid employee is going to regard your business and clients in the same meticulous and painstaking light that you will. So you'll probably have to lower your standards of quality and attention and plan to spend some time making up for the lack.

And with the rise in unlawful sexual harassment suits brought as the result of being fired, many rural entrepreneurs have been further discouraged from hiring help.

Many rural entrepreneurs advise that if you find an employee who is the exception to the rule, hold onto her as tightly as you can by increasing her pay, offering bonuses, and letting her know how much you appreciate her with added responsibilities and the occasional day off with pay.

When hiring employees, there are certain things you have to know. If you're hiring a person to work for you regularly, he will be considered to be your employee and you will have to deduct taxes, which you will have to file with the government either quarterly or once a year, depending on your tax setup.

Some businesses get around the process of withholding and payroll taxes by preferring to hire an employee as an independent contractor. This way, the contractor files a self-employment tax, which saves you a lot of paperwork. This works for such seasonal and periodic workers as gardeners and musicians, but it will send up red flags with the IRS if you try to hire a part-time office assistant in this way. If you do hire an independent contractor, if you pay them more than $600 over the course of a year, you must file a 1099 form on their behalf which reports their income.

No matter how you decide to "hire" an employee, make sure that you always communicate with them clearly and directly and immediately when there's a problem or complaint. And let them know when you think they did a job well done.

Working With Suppliers

When you're first starting out, you'll probably buy your supplies from stores and businesses you already have dealt with in the past.

Later on, as you grow, you might want to deal directly with whole-salers and commercial distributors, but even if your country business grow significantly in a short period of time, you still might prefer to do it all yourself.

The first issue you'll face when approaching suppliers is that they usually require large minimum orders so that they can keep their costs down. Their minimum might be more than you'll use in a month—or a year—and if you're dealing with perishable items, this can present an impending disaster.

When checking their prices, you might discover that their prices are actually higher than buying at retail, since they include the cost of delivering the supplies to you in their overhead. And, even for a distributor who deals in more than one type of supplies, your combined potential order might be too small for the company to want to deal with.

If you're like most rural entrepreneurs, in the beginning, you'll probably decide to do it all yourself. Some local businesses will allow you to set up a house charge account to simplify your bookkeeping and so that you can send a staff member to the market to pick up a few last-minute items and you don't have to dig up some cash and count the change you receive back. Some of these "suppliers" will also offer you a discount for buying in quantity and also for paying before net 30 days.

Even if you do it all yourself, however, it still pays to shop around. When buying office supplies, for instance, you'll probably spend the most at your neighborhood stationery store.

The next cheapest source will be a stationery superstore, though sometimes the quality and attention you'll receive is far below what you're used to. In my experience, the cheapest source of office supplies are the mail-order operations that ship the same day your order is received and offer large discounts on volume orders on top of their already low prices.

There are exceptions to everything, however, so the best advice is to take your time and shop around and don't be afraid to dicker. These companies want your business, and if you show you're going to be a good, steady customer, they'll work hard to keep you.

Understanding Taxes

When you first set up your country business and discover how much time, energy and paperwork you devote to taxes, you might wonder when you'll find the time to market your business and occasionally hold a client's hand. Between payroll and state taxes and your own income and other personal taxes, it can all seem pretty self-defeating at this point. Why go into business if most of your revenue will go towards taxes?

First of all, take a deep breath. It only seems overwhelming now as you're learning about your different responsibilities. Once you get the hang of it, recording and paying taxes—as well as figuring out your deductions—will turn out to consume just a small part of your bookkeeping and office time. As I mentioned earlier, this is why it's important to keep good records.

You will also be required to keep track of your revenue and expenses and to pay a tax to the Internal Revenue Service on any profit your country business earns. The amount of tax you pay will depend on the type of business you're running: a sole proprietorship or partnership, or a corporation. The tax structures for each differ.

Of course, since the startup costs in many country businesses are so high the first year or two, your expenses may exceed your income, so you won't have to pay tax. The IRS allows that there will be years when you'll earn no profit on paper, even though it assumes you are in business to earn a profit. As a result, many businesses claim a wealth of deductions to avoid showing a profit, and therefore, paying tax. That's why current tax law says that you must show a profit at least three years out of five to prove that you are running a viable business. If you show a loss three or more years out of the five, again, this will alert the IRS and set you up for the possibility of an audit.

As for payroll taxes, contact your state employment bureau about the exact deductions you should make for each employee, in addition to the federal tax bureau for information about income tax, Social Security, and other payroll taxes.

Country Business Profile
Specialty Food Business—Large Scale

Uncle Dave's Kitchen
Dave Lyon
Bondville, Vermont

Description of Business

A small food manufacturing company that sells one or products to stores and wholesalers. Most fall into two categories: elegant or homemade.

Ease of Startup

Difficult. You must go to your state department of agriculture to check out packaging and manufacturing requirements.

Range of Initial Investment

$10,000 is the absolute minimum.

Time Commitment

Full-time

Can You Run the Business From Home?

Yes

Success Potential

Difficult. There's a lot of competition out there.

How to Market the Business

Through publicity, tastings, trade shows, brochures.

The Pros

It's fun, and it's satisfying to get good feedback.

The Cons

It's a lot of hard work. Unless your product is different from what's already out there, your chances aren't good.

Special Considerations

For people who love to cook, turning a favorite recipe into big business can quickly dampen their enthusiasm.

For More Information

From Kitchen to Market by Stephen Hall (Dover, NH: Upstart Publishing, 1992)

Story of the Business

To a casual observer, Dave Lyon seems to have had the perfect life. He worked in manufacturing for a few decades before moving to Vermont to become a ski bum at the age of 50. He soon tired of that and went off to serve as president of Grolier International Publishing for a few years before he came back to Vermont again to "relax."

In the meantime, his wife was planning to start a specialty food business when their son—who was working for the Dukakis presidential campaign—fell into early retirement and came up to Vermont in 1989. "They wanted to make a new ketchup with no preservatives, made with honey and maple syrup instead of corn syrup," says Lyon. Dave Lyon decided to become involved in the company as Uncle Dave, figuring this would set the company apart from other specialty food businesses by backing the product up with a real person.

In the beginning, Uncle Dave's did a lot of grassroots marketing going to craft shows—one a week at the start—to exhibit the products. People would buy the ketchup and take it back to Minnesota—or wherever—with them. Shortly, Uncle Dave's would get a call from a small store in Minnesota placing an order.

After the ketchup hit the market, Lyon noticed a great need for quality pasta sauces. They developed spicy peanut pasta sauce, a Tex-Mex sauce and sundried tomato sauce. Like the ketchup, the pasta sauces have no preservatives and are all natural. Other products in the line now include mustard, honey and a Bloody Mary mix. The hardest part was getting the first distributor to agree to carry the ketchup.

"Sometimes we went to a supermarket and asked them to carry us. They'd contact a distributor because it's easier for them to order from the distributor than from us," explains Lyon. "Other times, we'd go straight to a distributor, show them our products and what we could do, backing this up with a real Uncle Dave. I volunteered to do demonstrations and to promote the product in other ways. This set us apart from the 2,000 other products they see every year."

The key is to have lots of distributors and to market a product that is different from all the others. "For instance, when we came out with pasta sauces, we came out with sauces nobody else had," explains Lyon. "Then we backed into marinaras, which other people did have. But once we had shelf space with the distributors, we could come out with other items because most distributors automatically take the new items their current producers bring out."

Lyon refers to the marketing strategy for Uncle Dave's as guerrilla marketing. His son works full-time to get publicity for the company. "Once we made the biggest Bloody Mary in the United States—350 gallons—using our mix," reports Lyon. Media mentions include favorable writeups in the Boston Globe, New York Times and Wall Street Journal. But all this doesn't come cheaply.

Though Uncle Dave's was launched with $10,000, that barely covered getting out the front door. The Lyons borrowed money from friends and investors by selling a minority interest in the company. They also got a loan from a bank via the Small Business Administration, which guaranteed 90 percent of the loan. "We asked for $250,000. By the time the paperwork was done, we needed another quarter million," he recalls. They got the loan after being in business for only two years. "Our enthusiasm helped, along with the fact that we had raised a quarter million on our own before that."

Today, Uncle Dave's grosses over a million a year, up from $100,000 the first year. Lyon acknowledges that not all aspiring specialty food producers want to become as large as Uncle Dave's. "If you just want to do the circuit with a small mail-order business and through craft shows and stores in Vermont, it's very easy," he

remarks. "I don't
know if you'll make any money, but in Vermont, it's a big cottage industry. When we started, there were only about 50 specialty food companies here. Today there are over 300."

Ideally you have to have a great cook on board. You'll need another person to work on marketing and someone to deal with distributors. Uncle Dave's has all three, but as Lyon puts it, his intention to relax in Vermont has gotten to the point where, he says, "I work 90 hours a day."

Don't say you haven't been warned.

Country Business Profile
Bed & Breakfast

Paisley and Parsley B&B
Bea Stone
Jackson, New Hampshire

Description of Business

A private house with a number of guest rooms to rent out overnight or longer to guests. Breakfast is served each morning.

Ease of Startup

Moderate. It's necessary to be licensed by the state. Make sure your home and guest rooms are welcoming to guests.

Range of Initial Investment

$10,000-$400,000.

Time Commitment

Full-time in season.

Can You Run the Business From Home?

Yes

Success Potential

Difficult. If you're in a tourist area, you'll do well, but don't expect to make your sole living from a B & B.

How to Market the Business

Guidebooks, advertising, national and local publicity, the Chamber of Commerce and the local bed-and-breakfast association.

The Pros

You'll meet interesting people who will envy your lifestyle.

The Cons

You won't have a lot of free time; it's more work than just making beds and cooking breakfast.

Special Considerations

For people who have a few extra rooms and who truly enjoy meeting all types of people, running a B & B will be a satisfying business.

For More Information

American Bed & Breakfast Association, 1407 Hugenot Road, Midlothian, VA 23113; *The Upstart Guide to Owning and Managing a Bed and Breakfast* by Lisa Rogak (Dover, NH: Upstart Publishing, 1994).

Story of the Business

"Everybody who comes to stay at our bed and breakfast tells us they want to live like we do," remarks Bea Stone.

She opened Paisley & Parsley, a three-room B & B in prime White Mountain tourist country in 1989. "It's the dream of most of our guests. But what they don't realize is they need a lot of energy and a background in cooking and entertaining in order to run a B&B. They also need to like living in a state of near-crisis and operating on a shoestring all the time," she adds. "If all those things are true, then I'd say this is the perfect business for them."

Stone and her husband are in an enviable position. When they retired, they sold their home in Mountain Lakes, New Jersey and used the proceeds to buy the house in Jackson. "For four years, we traveled every weekend looking for a house that would make a good B&B," she recalls. "We traveled from New Hampshire to North Carolina looking for an old house. Instead we ended up buying a new house with an incredible view of Mount Washington."

They decided on the new house because the rooms were spacious, and they didn't have to take down walls or redo plumbing fixtures, oven though the house hadn't been used previously as a B&B.

"Since we used money from the sale of our other house to finance it, there was no risk because we were going to live there anyway," explains Bea. "As a result, we feel we can take time off for ourselves. Someone with an incredible mortgage to pay might feel they wouldn't be able to do that."

Once they bought the house, they made sure the house met state safety codes; they had to install a hardwired smoke and fire alarm system. Then they were licensed to operate as a B & B by the state.

"We read some innkeeping books, found a good lawyer, an accountant and a bank. We joined the Chamber of Commerce and the local association of resort owners," she says. She also investigated places to advertise, the AAA, and the various inn and B & B guidebooks.

They've spent about $375,000 on the house, including the purchase and $25,000 for a new well.

"When we bought the house, we didn't know a new well was necessary, but fortunately we had the money for it," she says. "These are the kinds of things people need to roll with if they want to get into the business."

Bea also upgraded everything in the house. She bought brand-new beds, down comforters and beautiful linens. Her biggest expense has been the landscaping and developing herb and perennial gardens. "We're up to about $30,000 on the gardens alone," she remarks. She admits it's not necessary, but that it enhances the B & B. "It would have been pretty plain without it," she points out.

The Stones live in the house. This has its good and bad points, but they've managed to create their own private spaces. The busiest seasons are summer, fall foliage and February's peak skiing. Rooms range between $65 and $95 a night for a couple.

The breakfast is gourmet quality. Bea uses a lot of the produce from her gardens to prepare each meal. A typical summertime breakfast consists of mushroom crepes, fresh kiwi and strawberries and zucchini muffins.

The occupancy rate ranges between 50 and 75 percent. They get a lot of referrals from guests who have stayed there before. "Many people walk by when they're on vacation. They'll come in and book a weekend later in the season when they're up here again," she reports.

Bea hires a maid to work an average of 10 to 12 hours a week. She pays her $10 an hour, which is high for the area. She justifies it because that's what she paid a cleaning woman back in New Jersey.

The B&B grosses between $20,000 and $25,000 a year, and all profits are plowed back into the business.

"You have to really like people to do this," indicates Bea, "because you don't have a lot of free time. Having a good sense of humor also helps. When guests tell me they like what I've done, it's really good for my ego."

Country Business Profile
Used Bookstore

Lilac Hedge Bookshop
Bob Ericson
Norwich, Vermont

Description of Business

A store that sells used books, occasionally offering other merchandise such as records and antiques.

Ease of Startup

Moderate. Some people already have enough books to get started.

Range of Initial Investment

$15,000 for shelves, a storefront, and books.

Time Commitment

Full-time

Can You Run the Business From Home?

Yes

Success Potential

Difficult. Used bookstores are not as popular among the public as you might think.

How to Market the Business

Advertising, word of mouth, referrals.

The Pros

You'll meet a lot of interesting people. You can indulge your love of books.

The Cons

It's hard to make much money, especially when you exchange books.

Special Considerations

Book lovers who like to stay put and who don't need a lot of retirement income will do well running a used bookstore.

For More Information

How to Open a Used Bookstore, by Dale Gilbert (Dover, NH: Upstart Publishing, 1991).

Story of the Business

Book lovers are a breed just a bit different from other folk, but used book lovers are a species unto themselves, and you can spot them a mile away. Those with a particularly acute sense of smell can sniff them out, because their musty scent gives them away every time.

Bob Ericson opened the Lilac Hedge Bookshop in Norwich in 1983 with his late wife, Katherine. Years earlier, when they were living in Putney, Vermont, they opened the first Lilac Hedge, named for the row of lilacs that ringed the shop. When they heard about the impending construction of a new federal prison just down the road, they began to look elsewhere in Vermont.

They wanted to be surrounded by cosmopolitan people even though they were in the country, so they settled in Norwich, across the Connecticut River from Dartmouth College. "College towns are good places for book shops," he remarks. "We don't get a lot of students coming here, but just about everybody who got out of Dartmouth wants to come back to the area. A lot of them are readers."

The Ericsons originally got into the used book business because of their kids. "I'm a compulsive reader," says Bob. "When we sat down at breakfast, I read the labels on the cereal boxes. We always had a lot of books. We had so many that our kids said, 'Why not start a bookstore?'

So they did. Many people start out in the used book business buying books they like. However, according to Bob, there's one lesson you learn quickly if you don't want to starve. You find out that a lot of books you like don't sell at all.

"Normally, we sell a brand-new book for no higher than 50 percent of the published price, and probably only a quarter of that," he indicates. A book that sells for $20 new, he sells for four or five. "I hope people do keep buying new books because otherwise there wouldn't be any old books for me," he points out. "At used book-stores you find the good ones, since they've already been through a sorting-out process."

Bob does searches for customers, as do most old and new booksellers, but he likens the process to throwing bottles with messages into the ocean. He considers himself lucky if this one in four searches is successful. This isn't very hard to understand when he describes the desired books.

"I get asked to do searches on some very old, fairly esoteric philosophy books," he says. The most unusual search was for an ancient book on horses by a Byzantine writer. Another was for a copy of Alex Wilson's American Ornithology; he found a second edition of nine volumes, which he sold for $6,000-the most he's ever sold a book for.

Bob sells some of the paintings hanging in the bookstore and in the adjacent living room. He'll point out some other items for sale, like an oil lamp from the USS Constitution, an antique bed warmer and some wood carvings.

He doesn't live off the proceeds from the shop, which is located in a couple of rooms in the front of his house. He relies on pensions and other retirement income.

Chapter Six

Marketing Your Country Business

Marketing is frequently a term that makes many rural entrepreneurs uncomfortable. Marketing may conjure up images of expensive and ineffective ad campaigns as well as the feeling that there's something mystical about the ability to draw in customers on the strength of just words and/or pictures.

You don't need a degree in marketing to sell your business effectively. In fact, you're apt to sell it better than a professional, because you're not doing what everyone else is doing who's earned an expensive degree in marketing. After all, you know your business best. And if you're thinking of hiring somebody else to do it just to get the job off your hands, forget about it. Just as no one else will handle your customers like you will, so too you're the best person to promote your country business. After all, who else is better acquainted with it and therefore better able to convey the attachment and love you have for it to others?

Marketing can actually be fun. In fact, the more creative you are, the better—for you and your country business.

The Purpose of Marketing

You have a great product: your country business. But how will anyone hear about it unless you let them know you exist?

"Oh, they'll see my ads," you'll reply. As with any ad or notice that publicizes your country business, unfortunately only a tiny percentage of the people who see your advertisements will respond.

"Well, what about the chamber of commerce? I'm a member, you know." Yes, and so are 300 other businesses in your town, all seeking the same thing you are: customers.

Joining the chamber of commerce or other local business organization is a great idea, but they'll only do so much for you. After all, their role is to promote area businesses as one entity, and not individually.

"My brochure knocks 'em dead." But how are you going to get it in the hands of prospective clients in the first place? It's great if your brochure and other promotional materials really present an accurate and detailed picture of the products and services you offer. However, you must first get it into their hands.

The purpose of marketing is to develop and execute a number of different strategies that result in first having potential customers hear about your country business, and then convincing them to give you a try.

However, you must devote time and creativity to the marketing plan you developed in *Chapter Three: Planning Your Country*

Business. Always keep in mind that marketing in whatever form will help you to meet new customers—which will then turn them into repeat customers. Repeat business is the lifeblood of any country business, and the best thing about repeat customers, is the fact that getting them back incurs no additional marketing costs. They're already convinced of the value of your business, and you don't have to sell them on it over and over again.

Defining Your Customers

Americans are largely overwhelmed by media messages today. In addition, most of those messages have become quite specialized in addressing the audience the advertiser wants to reach.

You must do the same thing. You won't be able to reach everybody, and even if you could, your message is only one of thousands they see and hear every day.

The first step to reaching your customers is to target the kind of client you'd like to attract, even though a wider variety than you thought existed will eventually agree to do business with you. Keeping individual records about your customers from the beginning can help you to define your customer even more once you've been in business for awhile.

Defining your customer means you can then narrow down your choice of the avenues you have available to reach them, as well as the methods you use.

Ask yourself the following questions:

♦ What are three different types of customers you'd like to reach?

♦ Where will they come from?

♦ What is their income range?

♦ Why will become your customer?

♦ What do they require from your country business so that they keep coming back?

Finding Prospects

You have an idea of the kinds of customers who will be attracted to your country business. Now, how do you find them?

Through a variety of ways. You should know, however, that prospects are not the same thing as customers. In fact, only a small percentage of people who inquire about your country business and ask for or pick up your brochure will actually become your customer.

Despite this, you must view every prospect as a potential customer, but do not be disappointed when she decides not to do business with you. We have become a society of fishermen: because there is so much out there to chose from, we must know all there is about everything there is before we make a decision. And even then, there's a little voice in the back of our heads that says, "There's always something better."

Perhaps that is true. But you can help find and convert prospects into paying customers by concentrating on those avenues that your group of defined customers travel on.

Marketing is not always advertising, as many people wrongly assume. In fact, advertising is one of the least effective and most expensive ways to find your prospects.

Think about your defined customers and then consider the places you can find them.

Cloning & Keeping Good Customers

Once you get a good customer, hold onto him. Tight. The good news is, like that shampoo commercial where one person tells two friends and so on down the line, your own good customer knows other people who could also turn out to be good customers for you. After all, word of mouth is probably the most effective kind of marketing there is.

There are a variety of ways you can clone good customers. One way, if you send a regular letter or newsletter to your regular clients, is to ask them if they know of other people who would like to receive information about your country business.

Treating your repeat customers well each time they do business with you is in essence, a kind of cloning, since they are likely to come back again and again.

Some rural entrepreneurs report that up to 80% of their business comes from 20% of their customers. The best way to build up to this level and continue to clone other good customers is to a) continue to market to your targeted group of customers, and b) be consistent in maintaining the quality of your country business. After all, one of the reasons why customers come back is because they know what to expect.

Finding the Time

Finding the time to market their businesses is one of the biggest problems that many rural entrepreneurs have when it comes to marketing. The next time you say you don't have time to market your country business, consider these following words from one rural innkeeper who sets aside time to market her business every day:

153

"Time, of course, is the biggest marketing problem for country business owners. But if they knew how much business they could bring in, they might realize that some of the cooking and cleaning is best delegated to someone else, so they can make the time for serious marketing. To wit, here are the dollars we've billed in first-time business from recent national magazine coverage garnered through publicity, not advertising:

♦ *Country Living* (two-page spread): $82,400 over two years

♦ *Yankee* (13-page feature): $60,000 over the course of 18 months

♦ *Country Home* (eight-page feature): $23,300 over the course of fourteen months

♦ Total: $165,700

"Because of these figures, it's imperative to ask each customer or potential customer how you heard about us. This information should then be tabulated to determine your rate of return on paid advertising and where to spend more of your valuable time. Seeing exactly what you have billed from each of the previous year's directories/ads/listings makes the media-buying decisions much clearer. And it also becomes much easier to say *no* to pesky ad salesmen whose publications don't work for you."

Now consider some of the following ideas whenever you complain that you lack the time to market.

♦ A lot of marketing involves grunt work: stuffing envelopes, making lists, shuffling through ad rate cards. Do this during slow times of the day or night; it's easier to justify when ten other things aren't demanding your attention.

♦ Examine your slow times, whether it's every Monday or the month of March. Set up the following year's strategies by writing your marketing plan (see *Chapter Three: Planning Your Country Business*), and then perform maintenance tasks on your weekly slow day.

♦ Survey your staff for ideas. If it's appropriate, let them carry them out with your approval. Pay for all expenses, and hold a monthly contest for the best idea. They may surprise you.

♦ Here's a sneaky tip: Ask sales reps from different media to design a media plan for you as a way to get your business. Many reps will do this anyway, of course, giving the biggest percentage of the pie to themselves. Whether you follow through is up to you, but you'll get lots of suggestions and ideas for free and no time spent. Always ask about upcoming promotional tie-in events; frequently you'll get a reduced rate and increased exposure at the event as well.

♦ Hire someone to carry out your plan, if you truly can't find enough time, or let a staff member do it. One rural entrepreneur hired a PR consultant who was just starting out. She paid the consultant a below-market rate, but tied bonuses into any increased business that resulted from the additional publicity. Some country business owners say that novices are better than experts; although they don't have the contacts, they also don't have a lot of preconceived notions about what's right and what's wrong. With marketing, it's innovation that gets attention.

Advertising on a Budget

Advertising is a type of marketing where you pay for a certain amount of space or time so you can tell your message to a particular kind of audience. Since you're paying to send the message, you can say anything you want—time or space and money are the only factors that limit you.

Considering these limitations, advertising doesn't really give you much leeway. In fact, because you bought the space, you're obviously selling something, and most people turn right off when someone's trying to sell them something.

Take a look at the ads in your local newspaper or area magazine. What do they look like? How do they make you feel? Is there one in the entire publication that makes you want to drop what you're doing, pick up the phone and call?

Probably not. Do the same thing the next time you're watching TV or listening to the radio. Pay close attention to the locally-produced ads. Again, do they make you feel excited about whatever it is the advertiser is trying to sell?

I probably can predict what your answer will be. The vast majority of advertising in all media is placed to gain consumer awareness, to let people know that a business exists. And this type of advertising can attract customers to your country business—but very slowly. It's also hard to measure. How often do you go into a store and say that you heard their radio commercial? Unless the owner is a friend of yours, probably not.

Because advertising is so expensive, you can't waste money to use it just to let people know you're there. Publicity and other more direct marketing tools exist for this reason, and they're also cheap.

No, the only reason you should spend money to advertise is to back up a special promotion or discount that's you're offering for a limited time, or to offer customers a chance to respond to your ad and receive something for their efforts. A toll-free number, a discount coupon, or a special incentive will help you to measure how many people responded, and who then became one of your customers as the result of your ad. Then you can see if the ad paid for itself, and whether you should try another ad in a later issue of the magazine.

Some rural entrepreneurs report that they've felt pressure from a newspaper or magazine editor to advertise in exchange for a promise to cover their business in an editorial section of the publication. Though most editors will deny this ever happens, it does, and it's most likely to occur at smaller publications, where most or all of their revenue comes from advertising. And when the publisher also serves as the editor, you can be sure that any conflict of interest between advertising and editorial departments is frequently ignored.

If you do decide to advertise, don't settle for the quoted rate. Always ask, "Is that the best you can do?" Especially if the publication is nearing its closing date and there's still ad space left to fill, the sales rep or ad director might let it go at a significant discount. In addition, radio and TV stations and publications frequently offer a special rate to first-time advertisers in the hopes that they'll become regular advertisers. At other times, they'll offer a discount if you advertise in a special section or sponsor a certain program. Again, you should always ask.

Publicity

In the opinion of many rural entrepreneurs, publicity is the best kind of marketing there is, for aside from the initial costs of preparing a press release and contacting the media about your country business, publicity is free. And because when a writer writes up your business

157

in a magazine or newspaper, or a reporter gives you a glowing review on radio or TV, it is considered to be an endorsement of your business by that particular medium. You didn't pay someone to be mentioned, and the audience will respond more favorably to an unsolicited endorsement than to a paid ad.

As with defining your customer, you must also narrow down the media you wish to reach. Many times, your defined customer will select your media for you. For instance, you should target the media he is likely to read or listen to. Check the name of the editor on the masthead, or the names of one or two writers. Never contact the editor-in-chief of a large and/or frequent publication, since she will be far too busy to respond to you. The managing editor or an associate editor is a far better choice.

In any case, you will need to send your media contact your brochure, any other pertinent promotional materials, copies of other stories that have been written about you and your country business, and a cover letter and press release.

A cover letter should be short and to the point, and casual in tone. It also helps if you show you're familiar with the publication and the writer's work by mentioning a recent story. Try to highlight one thing that makes your country business different from other similar businesses in your area. After all, the editor probably gets bombarded with mailings from small businesses every day; his attitude about yours is probably going to be, "So what?" It's also a good idea to offer an angle for a story where the editor could fit you in. And so don't just send your brochure and press release. Tailor your letter to the editor and publication. This, more than anything else, will get the editor's attention.

Country Business Profile
Specialty Food Business—Small Scale

Spruce Mountain Blueberries
Molly Sholes
West Rockport, Maine

Description of Business

A business that produces specialty food products either fresh or prepared, sometimes even growing the ingredients.

Ease of Startup

Moderate. If you grow your own produce, it may take a few years to develop the crop.

Range of Initial Investment

$5,000, if you already have the land.

Time Commitment

Part-or full-time

Can You Run the Business From Home?

Yes

Success Potential

Difficult. The field is crowded. You need time to establish the product.

How to Market the Business

Advertising, trade shows, wholesalers, word of mouth, referrals.

The Pros

If you like to grow things and cook in bulk, this is a perfect business.

The Cons

There's not a lot of money in it. It's hard work to both grow and prepare your products.

Special Considerations

Retirees who like to juggle many different tasks and be tied to the homefront will be happy in the business.

For More Information

From Kitchen to Market by Stephen Hall (Dover, NH: Upstart Publishing, 1992).

Story of the Business

What Molly Sholes is doing today on her blueberry farm is the culmination of her experiences during her working life. She spent 19 years as a foreign service wife in India and Pakistan, working with natives to learn about their cuisine. She spent summers at a farm in Maine with a wolf, gas lights and 35 acres of wild blueberries. In 1986 she moved to the farm full-time and started her business. "I love the subcontinent, and I love blueberries, so I put the two together to form my business," she says.

Sholes has a value-added, integrated blueberry farm, which means she grows the blueberries and sells them to wholesalers to sell fresh-packed or to freeze. She also processes blueberries into six products from her home kitchen. She sells blueberry chutney, chutney with almonds and raisins, blueberry conserve, jam, whole berry syrup and vinegar. She works at the business year-round, but considers it a part-time occupation because in the winter she works as little as eight hours a week at the business.

"The combination of growing your own product and selling it in a packaged form is a wonderful country business because you can work both outside and inside," she reports. "Except for harvest season, which is July and August, I can pretty much work when I want."

During the harvest, Sholes has a workforce of ten people who rake the berries from the fields and then pick them over for foreign matter before packing them. In 1993 she grew 52,000 pounds of blueberries: 68 percent went to a commercial freezing company, 28 percent went to a fresh-pack wholesaler and four percent went into her freezer to make chutney the rest of the year. She also sells fresh blueberries to neighbors as a courtesy. The money she made is disproportionate, however: of her $40,000 gross, she brought in

$19,000 from selling the blueberries wholesale and $21,000 from selling her chutney.

She sells chutney direct to wholesalers—she prefers not to have a distributor or reps—and by mail order to her own list of 550 names. The wholesaler sells direct to retail outlets, gift shops and specialty food stores concentrated in the northeast. She hooked up with the wholesaler by exhibiting at trade shows and visiting specialty food stores. When she was beginning her business she did informal test marketing by bringing jars to people she knew at local businesses to see what they thought of her product.

"There's so much competition in every phase of this business that it pays to consult the Small Business Development Corporation or an equivalent service that's available," she says. Like other small states with cottage businesses, the state of Maine has drawn up a booklet for prospective specialty food producers, advising them to develop a marketing strategy and an enterprise budget. "None of which did I do," admits Sholes. Instead, she started out very small, putting a couple thousand dollars into the business each year; and she's stayed small. "If I lost money, it wasn't a disaster because I have enough money to live on from my retirement income," she adds. "I'm not trying to make a living; I'm trying to utilize the land in the best way I can."

Country Business Profile
Craftsperson

Marilyn Herman
Pomfret, Vermont

Description of Business

An individual who makes a particular line of crafts and sells them retail, wholesale, on consignment and at craft shows.

Ease of Startup

Easy, especially if you concentrate on craft shows.

Range of Initial Investment

$100 for supplies.

Time Commitment

Part-or full-time

Can You Run the Business From Home?

Yes

Success Potential

Moderate. The field is crowded; your products must stand out from the crowd.

How to Market the Business

By visiting shopkeepers, going to shows, having your own shop and using some word of mouth

The Pros

It's fun and easy. Most craftspeople run their business from home.

The Cons

It's highly competitive, shopkeepers can be condescending and there's not a lot of money in it.

Special Considerations

For people who always made crafts anyway and can be satisfied with the small amount of money it brings, give it a shot.

For More Information

Homemade Money, by Barbara Brabec, POB 2137, Naperville, IL 60567.

Story of the Business

Marilyn Herman has always been responsive to market trends when it comes to crafts. She spent a number of years making quilts for an artists' cooperative shop in Bar Harbor, Maine, when quilts were popular and reasonably priced. When there was a downturn in the demand for quilts, she switched to making crafts from birch bark and never looked back.

Even within her second crafts career, Marilyn has kept aware of the changes from year to year. She opened a shop next to her home. It was successful for the first two years, but she saw that her wholesale business was bringing in more money. Now she's thinking seriously about discontinuing the shop to concentrate fully on the wholesale end of the business.

That's the secret to being successful in the crafts business: anticipating what the market needs and then filling it. There are already too many people out there making knitted dolls, potholders and the like. When Marilyn started making birch baskets in 1990, she saw the burgeoning interest in anything remotely related to Native Americans would be popular. At the time there were only a handful of craftspeople who were making birch bark crafts.

"I did some experimenting with birch from trees on my farm. I learned about its malleability and the best time to harvest it," she recalls. She also collected sweetgrass and grapevine to use in the baskets. She sold them in her own shop and a few others in the area, including a shop in Woodstock, which has heavy tourist traffic. The manager at the Vermont State Crafts Center saw the baskets and placed an order. She's been busy ever since.

Marilyn makes a variety of crafts from the bark, including shelves, mirrors, baskets and canoes. The miniature canoes are her best-selling item. She collects the bark in June and July when the sap is running and the bark is most pliable. Then she weights it down to keep it flat; she stores the bark so she can use it year-round.

She ships her crafts to stores or delivers them herself. Stores take different commissions. In her area, if she sells on consignment, the store gets 30-35 percent; if they buy outright, they take 50 percent. Herman's baskets sell from $35 to $85 retail. Some shops prefer to buy the baskets wholesale, but Marilyn says you have to be careful. "They say they'll pay in 30 days, but lots of times it ends up being closer to 120," she remarks. When working with a new customer, Marilyn prefers to get paid when she delivers the order, and after she's developed a history with a particular store, she'll give more flexible terms.

Herman still sells quilted crafts like potholders and pillows to some of the local shops, but they specify what they want and she fills the order. She has a freer rein with her birch bark crafts.

Though she says she doesn't make a lot of money, she mentions a friend in Maine who supports her family on the $27,000 a year she makes from birch bark crafts. "Even she's found the market to be quite narrow, so she's expanded into jewelry and other products," Herman indicates.

Perhaps more than with other businesses, craftspeople must be versatile and willing to change in order to make a living. "It's a fun way to make a living," says Marilyn. "I'm compelled to make my crafts, I have to be creative. I'd rather do this than anything else."

Country Business Profile
Country Inn

West Mountain Inn
Wes Carlson
Arlington, Vermont

Description of Business

A multi-room inn open year-round with a restaurant open to guests and the public.

Ease of Startup

Difficult, if you're starting from scratch. Moderate, if you're buying an existing inn.

Range of Initial Investment

$300,000 to $1.5 million and up.

Time Commitment

More than full-time.

Can You Run the Business From Home?

Most innkeepers live on the premises.

Success Potential

Moderate. Location, ambiance and your dedication and hard work will determine whether you make it or not.

How to Market the Business

Through inn and travel guidebooks, hosting travel writers, publicity and regular mailings to repeat guests.

The Pros

The people.

The Cons

The hard work: it's not as easy as it looks. Also, innkeeping is a money-hungry business, whether it's for repairs, mailings or labor.

Special Considerations

For people who've always dreamed of being innkeepers and recognize the endless work it involves, the business can do quite well. If you can buy the inn outright, you'll live with a lot less stress.

For More Information

Independent Innkeepers Association, POB 150, Marshall, MI 49068, 800-344-5244.

Story of the Business

According to Wes Carlson, who's owned the 15-room West Mountain Inn since 1978, the best part of being an innkeeper is that the world comes to see you.

That's the most important part of having a country inn: the people. You've probably visited country inns on vacation and thought it looked easy. That's the first bubble you should break. The second is that because your guests are on vacation, they'll be on their best behavior and it will be easy to please them.

Truth is, if you don't absolutely love people, don't get into the business. The aura of hosting a country inn will wear off within the first week, and there, revealed in all its splendor, will be the 80-hour workweeks and, yes, the occasional ornery guest.

Wes Carlson was an elementary school principal in Hastings-on-Hudson in New York State when he retired to move to Vermont. "We had a friend who was trying to run the inn, and we came up to help him," Wes recalls. "My wife, Mary Ann, who was a teacher, could get a job up here and we were going to take life easy." As with most fantasies, the reality turned out to be quite different.

When they arrived, the inn was referred to locally as a bunch of "hippies on the hill" and Wes' friend was ready to bail out due to lack of business. After Carlson spent one summer at the inn, his friend did pull out—he was leasing the inn-and Carlson took over. He started by paying off the debts, cultivating repeat business and by working very closely with the town. "It worked out," he says. "We're pretty gregarious people."

He has innkeepers who take care of the day-to-day concerns, from taking reservations to ordering supplies and supervising housekeeping staff. Wes takes care of general management, but he takes it easy and lets his staff take care of things. "Basically, it runs itself," he says. "There are always nitty-gritty problems with the inn, but never anything that's totally insurmountable. Every one of our staff thinks it's their inn."

Why, in a field where burnout is almost inevitable after seven years of innkeeping, are the Carlsons still going strong? From the beginning, they decided what they wanted to do themselves and what they wanted to delegate to others. In an inn this size, with a number of staff, this is possible.

"Neither one of us were cooks, and we didn't like to clean," says Wes. "The main thing that helped is that we were out there with our guests. Many people who open inns today become so involved with cooking and cleaning and running the inn that they don't have time for their guests."

To look at the handsome, yet casual inn, it seems like it's had several large common rooms downstairs, and 13 rooms upstairs—all with private baths—since it was built back in the mid-19th century. Nothing could be further from the truth, and it's another reason why the Carlsons have longevity at the inn. They do a little expansion or improvement to the inn each year.

"When we came, there were only three shared baths for nine guest rooms," says Wes. Today, each of the 13 rooms in the inn and two more rooms in a house down the road has a private bath. "The expansion has been gradual, but we've maintained the ambiance." One year, the inn added a garden, another year, they added some llamas.

The Carlsons market the inn today through writeups in a few guidebooks, but say that their primary sales technique is word of mouth. "Caring for people is the main thing," says Wes. "The best person to come back is the customer you have right now. Treat them right, and they become regular customers." Each guest takes home an African violet and a chocolate llama, and a bowl of apples is found in each guest room.

The town hasn't used the phrase "hippies on the hill" in years. "We support the community," says Wes. The inn offers a high school scholarship to a local student who "works locally and thinks globally," as Wes put it. He also offers free meeting space to local nonprofit groups, which builds good will and helps the business.

Perhaps the main reason why Wes can kick back and combine a leisurely retirement with a bustling country inn is because the mortgage is paid off and the inn has a 70 percent occupancy rate year-round, which is high for the industry, even in Vermont. The inn is valued at $1.5 million, and grosses about $700,000 a year. The inn's busiest months are August and October, and is least crowded in April and May. From May 1st through mid-June of that first year, Wes says there might have been six couples who stayed at the inn. "Right now, we're considered to be one of the better inns in Vermont," he says. "Next time around, I want to retire at 21."

Chapter Seven

Financing Your Country Business

I recently spoke with a rural entrepreneur who had bought her business the previous year from a husband and wife who had owned the business for ten years. The previous owners decided to sell because they were burned out.

But that wasn't all. "She never kept any financial records at all," the new owner told me. And so, before buying the business, the new owner had to go through all of the country business's books to determine the business's annual income, and dig through ten years of pay stubs and cancelled checks to figure out the country business's approximate expenses. She says it only took a few days, but I figure after a short time, she got sick of it and just averaged costs and revenue for each year.

"I'm the type to keep records," she said, shaking her head. "I don't know how they did it."

Fortunately, she was able to piece together a financial picture of the business. Many rural entrepreneurs just guess when it comes to taxes, profit-and-loss statements, and cash flow. And if they ever want to sell the business, well, you see what happens is the prospective buyer wants to get an idea of the financial health of the country business.

It's not too difficult to keep a handle on the various financial aspects of running your country business. Take some time with it now and you'll spend less down the road.

Profits & Losses

One important way to gauge how your business is doing is to calculate a profit and loss statement. Even though money may be coming in regularly, it may be possible that you are losing money because your expenses exceed your income.

As I've said earlier, keeping accurate records will make figuring out your profit and loss statement much easier; all you have to do is plug in the numbers. There are two kinds of profit and loss statements you can keep: one that projects your estimated profits and losses, and another that keeps track on a weekly or monthly basis to help you see how well your country business is doing. You can also compare the two, and if your projections are either 20% higher or lower than your actual figures, based on seasonality, this method will enable you to adjust your projects profit and loss statements as you go along.

First, figure out your business's gross revenues for the year, including fees and payments for all products and services, as well as any interest income and commissions. Next, get out the list of operating costs you drew up in *Chapter Five: Operating Your*

Country Business, and again, using either actual figures or estimates, add up all of your expenses for the year. You'll include salaries, the mortgage and utilities, business loans, office expenses, and everything else that applies to your country business.

And don't forget about depreciation. Ask your accountant for advice on this, but chances are that you'll be able to deduct the amount that is deemed to depreciate on your house, office equipment, and other big-ticket items this year. This is not strictly an expense, but will serve to help lower your profit, which will then lower your tax bill.

Also, don't forget about the interest you pay on any loans connected with the business. And remember that the type of business you run—sole proprietorship, partnership, or corporation—will also affect your profit and loss statement.

After deducting all of your expenses from your revenue, you'll be left with a pretax profit or loss. There's one more step, though. Now deduct all of the taxes you pay in connection with your business—except payroll taxes, which are figured into your payroll expenses—and you will come up with your actual net profit or loss, which probably seems a long way from your initial gross revenue figure.

Though you'll always have certain fixed expenses, there are a variety of ways you can adjust your profit and loss statement: reducing your expenses, raising rates and fees, and increasing the marketing you do, to name just a few.

Over time, you will be able to see which features at what brings customers back, and those that don't matter. Running a country business is a constant experiment; your profit and loss statement is a constant reminder of how well your experiment is doing.

Keeping Track of Your Money

Most rural entrepreneurs use a variety of methods to help them keep track of their money, both revenue and expenses.

The basic record will probably be your checkbook. There are a number of business checking accounts that come with built-in ledgers where you can record your expenses under different expense categories at the same time you write a check. Separating these expenses in advance makes it easy at the end of the year to determine how much you've spent in each category, and if you need to cut back.

Many country business owners prefer to keep their financial records on computer with a program like Quicken or QuickBooks. This software helps you to keep track of your expenses and separate them into categories, add them up in a flash, and even write checks on your computer printer.

Whatever method you choose, make sure that it's easy to use and that you check in with it at least once a week. Going longer than that will make keeping track of your money a chore and something you're likely to put off, which will make it more likely that you'll make mistakes.

Fortunately, some of the companies that you'll do business with are making it easier for their customers to keep track of their money. Credit and charge card companies now offer a breakdown of charges in different categories on their monthly statement. Some of the suppliers with which you maintain an account will also provide this service. And if they don't already do this, ask. They might start.

Developing Your Credit

If you're in business for any length of time, you're going to need credit in one form or another. Most of the time, it will be from suppliers who deal with you on a regular basis and who don't deal in picking up cash or checks with each delivery they make. Not only is it too unwieldy and increases the possibility of loss, it's a big waste of time.

But most suppliers and other companies won't offer you credit unless you've done business with them before. It's the age-old Catch 22: how can you develop your credit if no one will give you any in the first place?

Fortunately, there are ways around this. Many companies will open a credit line for you based on your personal credit record. They'll usually start you out small, and then increase your credit line as your history with them grows. Needless to say, you'll help your credit line if you always pay promptly, even before the due date, and by acting promptly whenever they or you have questions about your account.

With other suppliers, you'll need to prove yourself in the beginning, and your personal credit, no matter how stellar, will have nothing to do with it. These companies will make you pay cash or by check before they deliver the goods, and only after a certain period of time will they begin to extend you credit, and only a little at a time at first.

Once you begin to establish a credit record with your country business, you'll undoubtedly be solicited by charge card companies that invite you to open a business account with a high credit limit and low monthly payments. Though having a business credit card account helps in many instances—such as renting a car or buying airline tickets in certain situations—try not to use them too much. When cards are almost universally accepted, because it's easier to slap down the plastic than to apply for a basic account with a supplier, you might be tempted to run up huge bills with their inherent high interest charges. This is a high price to pay for apparent convenience. Instead, use them sparingly, appreciate them for what they are—an extremely expensive way to borrow money—and be as judicious with their use and payment as you are with your other creditors. After all, they can help develop your credit rating, too.

And although banks can be picky about lending money to people who have no experience running a business, you might apply for a line of credit at your bank, that is, if you don't have one already. Learning to rely on it only in emergency financial situations, then paying back the money immediately will help your business get through the tough times, and you will have them.

Working With Suppliers

As I've already said, one part of working with suppliers is to build up credit, and a working relationship. There are other ways as well.

Getting the best price may be the most important thing to you. Other rural entrepreneurs might be attracted by a company's twice-weekly delivery schedule, while still others might favor a supplier because of the particular brands the company carries.

Most suppliers will bend over backwards to get your business, though you may find that you'll have to jump through a few hoops at first, for instance, to get a credit account set up in your initial dealings with the company.

There are many ways to find the suppliers who will work with you and who you'll feel most comfortable working with. You should know if one supplier doesn't give you the terms you'd like, there are others who will. Don't sign on with one right away; instead, take the time to shop around for the best price, the quality you want, and the working relationship you feel comfortable with. Whether you prefer to deal by mail, have the items delivered to your door, or pick them up yourself, it's easy to find the best supplier for your country business.

Borrowing Money

The issue of borrowing money in these credit-weary days is apt to be a sticky one with rural entrepreneurs who may have to take out a first or second mortgage to buy an existing country business or to start one from scratch. "I'm in enough debt already," you may say, "Why would I want to borrow any more?"

As you'll see in an upcoming section later in this chapter, sometimes your cash flow won't keep up with your expenses. Even if you and/or a partner holds down a steady job, trust me when I say there will be times when that won't be enough. Operating and maintaining a country business with all of the expenses that continue steadily from month to month will eat up huge amounts of cash, and during those times, it may be necessary to borrow money.

If you have a rich relative or a sizable trust fund, you can skip over this section. But if you're like most of us, you'll need to rely on a conventional financing source. And since you already know to anticipate these cycles, you should take steps now to line up an available source of credit that you can draw upon immediately.

I know of many examples where rural entrepreneurs have drawn on their credit cards to initially finance their businesses, and then have gone back to them when things get slow. At anywhere from a

12 to 21% annual rate of interest, it's a very expensive way to borrow money. Even if you fully intend to pay it back before interest has a chance to accumulate, there will be times when you are only able to make the minimum payment.

Some rural entrepreneurs form partnerships just for this reason: to have a silent partner with deep pockets who's looking for a good rate of return on his money. But if you prefer to have a partner for other reasons—or to go it alone—and you don't want to have to rely on your credit cards, there is another option, and that is to open a line of credit at your bank.

If you don't want to go this route, or get turned down for it, there is the old-fashioned way, and that is to save for a rainy day. When business is booming and revenue is strong, set aside a certain percentage—some say 20% of your gross revenue—and sock it away in an interest-bearing savings account. Don't invest it in a place where you don't have instant access to your funds. Even though the interest rate may be less, you'll probably pay more by paying a penalty for early withdrawal from an IRA, mutual fund, or other investment. A money market fund is best; the interest rates tends to be a little higher than a passbook savings account, and you have immediate access to your money.

How to Give Credit to Customers

Aside from billing with payment due in 30 days, which is standard business procedure, the primary way that most businesses extend credit to their customers is by accepting the several major types of credit cards that are popularly used today. MasterCard, Visa, American Express, and Discover are accepted by many country businesses, whether they're mail-order or retail establishments. The credit card companies will charge a fee to set you up with their service, and then you'll pay the company a percentage of every transaction made by a customer, usually two to five percent. Your account is typically credited within one to three days after you enter a transaction into the system, and there are certain restrictions each company places on its members. It is relatively simple to apply for privileges that will allow you to accept credit cards from your patrons.

However, some rural entrepreneurs decide not to accept charge cards from their customers. Either their volume is too low to justify paying the commissions, or else the credit company places too many restrictions on them. Some have also said that the companies tend to have a patronizing attitude towards smaller companies—such as new country businesses—because they simply don't provide the commission revenue that larger businesses do.

The most important reason for a country business to accept credit cards is to make it easier for your customer to pay you. So even if you hate the idea of credit cards, you should definitely arrange to accept them. It may be money in someone else's pocket if you don't.

Any way you decide to extend credit to customers, it's important that you do offer it in some form. We have a love-hate relationship with it as a society, however, but since we do rely on it, you should arrange to be able to accept it before you open your country business.

Improving Cash Flow

Even though your country business will be a business where the cash flow will be highly erratic at times, you can, to some extent, predict when your cash flow will slow down and when it will be high. This will help you to see which months you should stockpile some of your excess cash in order to provide you with cash flow and income in the down times.

Cash flow is defined as the pattern of movement of cash in and out of a business: revenue and expenses. If you apply for a loan with a bank or other financial company after your business is up and running, you'll have to provide an analysis of your cash flow; if you're just starting out, you may be required to provide the loan officer with a projected cash flow statement.

Cash flow includes all actual monies coming in and going out of the business, and includes cash, checks, and revenue from credit cards. Depreciation does not factor into your cash flow analysis.

The first step to improving your cash flow is to increase your business year-round. But the effects from this aren't always that immediate, and there are thing you can do to even out your cash flow a little more.

Tying in with your own cash flow projections, you might want to conduct special promotions during the times of the year when your cash flow needs boosting the most. Another way to even out your expenses and therefore improve your cash flow is to ask your utility companies to average out your payments so that you basically pay the same amount each month year-round. And as I suggested earlier, if you stash away 20% of your gross revenue during the busy times, you'll have money to draw on during the slow months.

Country Business Profile
Restaurant

Brannon's
Nancy Brannon
Cody, Wyoming

Description of Business

A seasonal, limited-menu restaurant that's open only two nights a week.

Ease of Startup

Difficult. It takes money, vision and persistence.

Range of Initial Investment

At least $50,000 to start; it's easy to spend $200,000 and up if you purchase the property.

Time Commitment

More than full-time in season.

Can You Run the Business From Home?

No

Success Potential

Moderate. If you stress quality and atmosphere in an area where these things are rare, you'll build a following.

How to Market the Business

Publicity, advertising and attention to the community will create word of mouth and regulars, the lifeblood of a restaurant.

The Pros

Every evening, the curtain goes up: you and the food are the stars.

The Cons

Be prepared to work twice as hard as you think you need to.

Special Considerations

If you limit your restaurant to a couple of nights, or one meal, two people can handle it by themselves. Beyond that, you have to hire help.

For More Information

The National Restaurant Association, 1200 17th St. NW, Washington, DC 20036; *The Restaurant Planning Guide,* by Peter Rainsford and David H. Bangs, Jr. (Dover, NH: Upstart Publishing, 1992).

Story of the Business

Nancy Brannon—an expatriate from Columbus, Ohio, and the advertising business—had been living in Cody, Wyoming, for a short time when, in the space of two months, she met a man, married him and bought an abandoned lodge 3-1/2 miles up a remote dirt road. While they were on their honeymoon, they planned what would become Brannon's, a gourmet Italian restaurant that serves an eight-course Italian feast on Friday and Saturday nights, March through October.

"A honeymoon is the perfect time to come up with something like this because you're floating three feet off the ground," relates Nancy. Reality struck when they got back. They started removing the masses of garbage from inside and out of the main lodge, repairing the burst pipes and broken windows and replacing the roof. Her sister, who had lived in Cody for a few years longer than Nancy, thought she was crazy. "The forest service even had plans to burn the building, it was so bad," Nancy admits.

That was in 1983. Today, Brannon's has served people from 28 countries and all 50 states, and it's necessary to make reservations three to four months in advance. The restaurant has been written up in *Bon Appetit, Family Circle* and many other publications. Nancy has published two cookbooks and is working on two more. She also has a line of specialty foods that sells in stores throughout the region.

What happened to make Brannon's such a desirable restaurant? Endless hard work, along with a special vision about exactly what people are going to get from your restaurant: The food, the service and the atmosphere are equal partners. Nancy prepares and cooks all the dishes, while her husband, Dave, serves.

"We decided on the feast format because you can prepare many dishes in advance," says Nancy. They chose Italian because it's a limitless cuisine. "We figured if we didn't get bored, our guests wouldn't either. If I had to stand here and slap tomato sauce on everything that left the kitchen, I'd be bored to tears."

The menu changes frequently; Nancy relies on her collection of more than 300 Italian cookbooks for inspiration. She also subscribes to Italian food magazines and has learned enough Italian to read the recipes. "We gear it toward foods that are seasonal," she indicates. "We start with two entrees on each menu and build the feast from there."

There is only one sitting each night because the feast can last more than four hours. There are intermissions between a few of the courses called pausas; guests can take their wine and wander outdoors by the creek or in front of the fireplace. The atmosphere is in keeping with the theme. Italian music and wine complements the feast and the lighting is provided by kerosene lamps. Brannon's only books a maximum of five tables per night.

Nancy estimates she spends 50 hours a week working at the restaurant part of the business, She does some food preparation on Wednesday and spends all day Thursday on prep. Then on Friday and Saturday, she easily works 14-hour days. There are five cabins where guests can stay overnight. In the morning, Nancy has a breakfast basket waiting for her guests. The baskets are filled with pastries, fruit, juice, coffee and flowers.

The price tag for spending the night at Brannon's is not cheap. The feast is prix fixe at $49 per person; wine and beverages are extra. A cabin starts at $75 per night for a couple. In the beginning, even though there were many nights when there were only one or two couples for dinner, they knew the restaurant would eventually succeed. An article in a Montana newspaper put them on the map that first year; since then, word of mouth has carried them.

"Don't do it unless you love the work and long hours," advises

Nancy. "You really are married to the business."

Today Brannon's grosses about $100,000 each year, with food costs hovering around 27 percent. But it hasn't been easy.

"The night before we opened, we were still hanging pictures," remembers Nancy. "When we had finished, we turned on the music, lit the lamps and just stood there and cried. It wasn't just what we had envisioned, it was better. When our guests go home, they write us thank you notes and send us gifts. And of course, they come back."

Country Business Profile
Small Scale Farming

Darby Brook Farm
Howard Weeks
Alstead, New Hampshire

Description of Business

A single-product or multiproduct farm of 10 acres or less that can be handled by one or two people with a minimum of outside labor.

Ease of Startup

Easy. All you need are some seeds and determination.

Range of Initial Investment

$100-$300 for seeds and handtools, if you already own the land. If not, the cost of land varies widely and depends on where you live.

Time Commitment

Minimal in winter; full-time in summer

Can You Run the Business From Home?

You'd better.

Success Potential

Moderate. The more products to fall back on, the better, given the vagaries of climate and consumer demand.

How to Market the Business

It's important to stay local. Word of mouth, roadside stands, restaurant accounts, gourmet and tourist shops, farmer's markets.

The Pros

It's extremely satisfying.

The Cons

You won't get rich; you might break even. Farming is hard work.

Special Considerations

For weekend gardeners who've always wanted to spend the summer in the garden, this is a perfect business.

For More Information

Local agricultural extension offices; Natural Organic Farming Association; *The New Organic Grower* (Chelsea Green) by Eliot Coleman; *Organic Gardening Magazine*.

Story of the Business

Given its short growing seasons, northern New England might not seem the ideal place to go into business as a farmer. However, the condensed time frame and a few acres make a perfect retirement business for someone who enjoys gardening and wants to turn it into a part-time livelihood.

Howard Weeks, 67, has been farming a two-acre plot in the southwest corner of New Hampshire for 11 years. He cultivates assorted vegetables like broccoli, cabbage and eggplant. He also has pick-your-own strawberry and raspberry patches. A 10-acre hayfield provides extra income. Locals come to the house and buy produce directly from him. He also sells produce once or twice a week at a farmer's market in Keene, 10 miles south. To provide extra income and to make productive use of his 10-room 200-year-old farmhouse, he also runs a small bed & breakfast business in the summertime.

"Things all fall together in your life sometimes," says Weeks, explaining how he moved to New Hampshire and started farming. "I'd been working as a furniture designer in New York, where I grew up, but I spent my summers here in New Hampshire on a farm my father bought in 1929. In 1981, my brother and I inherited the farm, but since he didn't want it I bought him out and moved here full-time.'

Once he left New York, Weeks attended horticulture classes at the University of New Hampshire for two years before he began to farm. "Since I had inherited the farm, I felt I should learn something about taking care of it. I used some savings to go to school. It was very beneficial."

Even though he had kept a garden when he lived in New York, it was only after attending UNH that Weeks felt he knew enough to start. He started out small. First he put in the apple orchard, which wouldn't bear fruit for several years. Then he put in the raspberries; they began to generate income the first summer. Then he put in the vegetable garden. Two years ago he started selling at the farmer's market; he usually sells everything he brings. "I don't hire people to help me because my operation is too small," he explains. "Then I'd have to pay worker's compensation and taxes, and that's a little overwhelming. One of the reasons I don't expand is because the farm isn't big enough. Besides I can handle everything by myself." He does, however, hire a helper four hours a week to clean the house when the B & B is in operation.

Off-season Howard designs the garden and starts seedlings in his tiny A-frame greenhouse. He also makes furniture and does cabinet-work for local people. Last winter he built a barn to store hay. In-season between the farm and the B & B, Weeks keeps busy. Work on the farm naturally spaces itself out. "I'm pretty busy from May until October; at least the fruits and vegetables are harvested at different times." The orchard is harvested late in the season. Weeks turns most of the apples into cider, which he sells from his house.

He has experimented with some marketing techniques to increase business, but is quick to discontinue them if they don't pan out.

"I tried a roadside stand, but it didn't seem to work—the produce wilted as it stayed out there all day. Anyway, people know to come to the farm if they want vegetables because I'll pick them right here.

"Last year, I tried providing specialty crops for neighbors. People came here every week to get vegetables. I would pick root crops like carrots for them. I'd dig them up every week and have them ready for pick up. People liked that. so I'm planning to promote that more this year."

His marketing is on a small scale. There's free publicity in local newspapers, by word of mouth and at the farmer's market. He is thinking about building a larger greenhouse to increase the length of his growing season. "For now, plastic covers extend the season, and plants tend to survive longer. A larger greenhouse would be a plus because I could get started sooner and set my prices lower because my volume would increase.

"But if you're looking for a business to retire and make a lot of money, this isn't it," warns Weeks. "It's a lot of work. If you have a feeling for plants and like to work outdoors, it's a great business. It's exciting when something you've planted comes up, and it's also a pleasure when you can eat something you've grown. My aim is to supply the needs of local people. "

The pluses? If you already have the land, the initial investment is low. "If you can just buy the seeds, you can start," indicates Weeks. He spends about $100 on seeds every year, and another $100 to replace the raspberry and strawberry plants. "I do almost everything by hand because I stay small. Buying a lot of equipment can kill you."

But so might the gross, which Weeks estimates to run from $1,500 to $2,000 a season. His farm is certified organic by the state, but his small size might interfere with his rating. New Hampshire is planning to change the rules in 1994, denying certification to organic growers who gross less than $5,000 a season.

But that doesn't bother Weeks. "Neither the B & B nor the farm could supply me with a living alone, but for people who want to live in the country and work outdoors it's a great way to live. I'm 67 and wondering how long I'll be able to farm. Even though I'm retired, I feel it's important to keep productive."

Country Business Profile
Cake Maker & Decorator

Barbara Stinson
Hanover, New Hampshire

Description of Business

An individual who makes custom decorated cakes for special occasions that are sold through stores or by word of mouth.

Ease of Startup

Moderately easy. You should get some training. You will have to buy the equipment and ingredients, then publicize your business.

Range of Initial Investment

$250-500 for pans and ingredients.

Time Commitment

Part-time

Can You Run the Business From Home?

Yes

Success Potential

Easy. Skilled cake decorators are in demand, especially in areas without a bakery.

How to Market the Business

Advertising, publicity, word of mouth, referrals.

The Pros:

It's a happy business, and it's creative.

The Cons

There might not be enough demand in your area for you to rely solely on the income.

Special Considerations

A person who likes to stay at home and doesn't mind receiving orders on short notice will do well.

For More Information

Cake decorating course at community schools or through the Wilton Cake Decorating Company, Wilton, Connecticut.

Story of the Business

Barbara Stinson got into the cake business by default. She and her husband, Jack, had recently opened a general store. About a year into the business, they bought a freezer so they could sell ice cream.

The ice cream didn't budge. Barbara was still teaching psychiatry at the nearby Dartmouth-Hitchcock Medical Center when her secretary brought in a couple of cakes she had made. They were beautiful and delicious. Barbara decided to hire her secretary to make cakes on the side to encourage people to buy the ice cream.

After awhile, the secretary's prices increased and she wanted to make just two a week. The business was demanding two a day. "I decided I had to do the cakes, or get someone else to do them," remembers Barbara. Since she couldn't find anyone to make them, she decided to do it herself. She spent a day with a known cake decorator in a nearby town, and then started making the cakes for the store.

"After I learned how to make flowers and do the edging, we put a couple of them in the window. The business increased to the point where I left my job," she says.

The Stinsons make all their cakes from scratch. "I convinced Jack to be the baker because he's an engineer and much more precise than I am. I do the decorating," she remarks. "Our success is due to the fact that we make the cakes from scratch; they're not fluff cakes."

They make the cakes at home because there wasn't room in the store and because their office is in their home. "It was natural for Jack to work in the office, so when the buzzer went off, he'd take them out of the oven. When I got home, I'd decorate them," she says.

They make the most cakes—mainly white and yellow cakes—in summer because people don't want to be bothered with a hot oven. In the wintertime, chocolate cakes are popular. Sixty percent of their cakes are for birthdays, wedding cakes make up 30 percent of demand, and all-occasion cakes account for about 10 percent of their business.

The Stinsons charge $13 for an 8-inch one-layer cake, and $15 for a 10-inch cake. She concentrates on single-layer cakes because she's a perfectionist. With two layers, there's a distinct line that separates the two layers. With sheet cakes, she puts the cake on plywood boards covered with aluminum foil to prevent the cake from cracking, as it tends to do on cardboard. An 11 x 15-inch sheet cake is $25, and a 12 x 18-inch cake is $35; a carrot cake with cream cheese frosting costs $7 more.

Barbara suggests that a person who wants to get into the cake business start by offering to serve as backup help. "I've tried to find someone to make them for me, when I'm busy or tired," she indicates. "Cake decorating is somewhat demanding. If I look at the cake book and see I have to make five cakes on Friday, I know I'm not going out that day."

She can decorate a cake in seven minutes. Her record is 27 cakes in one day. The occasion? Valentine's Day. "After that, I had tennis elbow for a week," she laughs.

Chapter Eight

Growing Your
Country Business

Growing a business today can be a challenge. Though everything you will do as a rural entrepreneur will in some way influence how your business grows, most of the time your thoughts will not be on growth, but on putting out all of the little fires that will pop up each day. If you have any time or energy left at the end of the day to think about growth, it may be along the lines of how to slow it down so that you'll have at least 15 minutes each day to call your own.

Seriously, growth—or the lack of it—is an issue that every rural entrepreneur has to face sooner or later. This chapter will show you how to deal with the variety of ways that growth will manifest itself in your country business. The good news is if you've gotten this far in your determination to start your country business, handling growth will probably turn out to be the least of your troubles.

The Problems of Business Growth

Many rural entrepreneurs feel that of all the business problems to have, those that involve issues of growth are among the easiest to handle.

It's not always so, however, Though growth as a rule means increased revenue and business, it also means more work and expenses, as well as more headaches to deal with.

Some country businesses will grow at a slow steady rate of 8 to 10% a year. Others will explode after a glowing article in a large-circulation magazine or newspaper appears. Which is better? While some prefer slow growth as a way to allow them to learn about the business and grow into it, others say that rapid and/or sudden growth provides them with a real education of what running a country business is all about, and provides a needed boost to the business when the owner might have otherwise been hesitant about forging ahead. This kick in the pants is sometimes exactly what a rural entrepreneur needs.

Growth can be managed and controlled to some extent. How you do it and whether you do it is up to you. One issue you'll face with a growing country business is whether or not to hire employees, or, if you already have help, whether you should increase their hours to full-time or hire more workers.

Your country business is your baby, and if you're used to doing it all yourself you may find it hard to delegate some of the responsibility to someone else, even if it means more free time for you. Many rural entrepreneurs have difficulty letting go at first, but with time and as you begin to see the high level of the ability of the people you do hire, you will trust in them more, which will leave you with time to turn to other problems in the business that need to be addressed.

Another by-product of growth is what to do with the extra

money. Some rural entrepreneurs use it to pay off some of their personal and business debts, but the IRS will count these monies as personal income. It's best to do this over time, though some people feel that the savings you'll make in not paying debt interest will more than offset the increased tax you'll have to pay.

How to Solve Business Problems

Every day that you're running your country business, you will run into problems. Some will be easy to remedy while for others, you will need help, either in the form of paid staff or good advice from other rural entrepreneurs who have been through it all already.

With some problems, you'll be so busy that you won't have time to think about your options. You'll dig right in then and there and do whatever it takes to get the job done.

Building up a good relationship with other country business owners in your area is a great way to have a network of experienced people who've probably already been through for what you currently need advice. In turn, they will turn to you at some point in the future for your advice and help with something as well.

They won't be able to answer all of your questions or provide solutions to every problem, however, For that, your local or regional chamber of commerce and small business networks may help, at least in terms of broad or specific advice.

In fact, you'll find a ready number of people who you already deal with who are able to work with you to help you solve the problems that are unique to your business. Your accountant can also help you determine how one capital improvement to your country business and the projected income it will bring will affect the taxes you'll have to pay next year.

Your banker can also help you with your business problems, as well as your lawyer, your realtor, and other rural entrepreneurs in your area. In fact, just when you think that there's no one you can turn to for help for your business, if you look around, you'll discover a surfeit of people ready and willing to help you—and most of the time, the advice will be free.

No matter what kind of brick wall you'll come up against in running your country business, you will be able to find help.

Managing Employees for Efficiency

The art of management once prescribed that the boss or manager rule with an iron grip in one hand and a whip in the other. Just like any strict disciplinarian parent, both employer and employee knew who was in charge. The employee went along with this facade, but more often than not, managed to get away with things whenever he could, and did only what was expected of him, and never anything more.

The opposite philosophy was that of the sensitive manager. He soft-pedaled harsh news, coddled his employees, and always was ready to heap lavish praise at the tiniest accomplishment. Again, employees went along with it, but felt they were never fully trusted or appreciated for their own talents and efforts. As before, quality and morale suffered.

The ideal management style for a small country business is to let employees feel as though they are responsible for the business's success or failure; that is, they treat it as though it were their own, which comes with certain privileges *and* responsibilities.

This style is perfect for rural entrepreneurs who need to delegate, and also because employees at a country business tend to very quickly develop a personal relationship with the boss. The type of management that's required may run counter to what many people think being a boss ought to be, but in the end, you'll find that your employees will be happier, more productive, and will also stay with you longer if you learn to manage them in this way.

It's not easy to do this, however, People who feel they have to control their employees in order to get them to work may run into problems with executing this altered style of management. However, once you see that your employees will treat your business almost as well as you do, it won't take long for you to become a proponent of this management style and actually begin to adopt in in other areas of your life.

Here's how to do it. Say you need to hire an employee to work 20 hours a week at your country business, helping out wherever you happen to need it. First, determine the tasks she says she's best at, and which of those she would feel comfortable being left alone to execute.

Train her by going through the various tasks she'll need to become familiar with, from answering the phone to keeping the books. Have her watch you do it a few times, and then let her go off to do it yourself. Assure her that she can approach you with any questions she has, no matter how trivial they may seem to her. Encourage her to maintain open communication with you at all times. Your end of the deal is to remain open to her queries and always respond in a patient manner. Then, once it appears she has one task down pat, send another her way.

If she makes mistakes, call them to her attention immediately, and then patiently and without judgment, explain to her the way to do it that's best for the business and why. Make sure that it's not just because she's doing the tasks a bit differently from how you would to it. In fact, for maximum efficiency, try not to get too caught up with how things get done, rather, that they *do* get done. If you insist that your employees follow certain steps in order to reach the final solution, you'll find that you'll be trying to squeeze a lot of round pegs into square holes. The outcome may turn out the same, but the morale may not, and your efficiency will, as a result, probably drop.

Then, as her responsibilities grow, increase her pay based on her performance and give her regular bonuses and days off with pay. The idea is for her to feel personally responsible for the happiness of your—and *her*—customers so that your time is freed up to work on other projects without worrying about the business.

The secret to successfully managing employees is to show them what to do, trust that they'll do it, and then leave them alone. Though many employees will be taken aback by this unique approach, and some will find it to be too alien for their tastes, the great majority will meet the challenge and help to build your business while cultivating a personal relationship with you.

In the end, running a country business can be one of the toughest but most rewarding things you can do in your life. Even during your most jam-packed days, try to remember to have fun along the way and keep in mind why you chose the rural place where you live.

Country Business Profile
Second-Hand Clothing Store

Patricia Owens
Pat Owens
South Strafford, Vermont

Description of Business

A shop that sells quality used clothing.

Ease of Startup

Easy. There's more clothing out there and people who want to sell it to you—than you'd imagine.

Range of Initial Investment

$0-$2,000. Fixing up the space can cost a few hundred dollars. If you only sell clothing on consignment, inventory will cost you nothing.

Time Commitment

Full-time

Can You Run the Business From Home?

No

Success Potential

Easy. You'll do well if you're selective about the clothes you choose to sell, making sure they're fashionable and clean.

How to Market the Business

Your own house-generated mailing list, word of mouth, advertising.

The Pros

Perfect for people who love clothes.

The Cons

You'll spend a lot of time cleaning and mending clothes before you put them out to sell.

Special Considerations

It's important to have a theme to your store; this is what will impress customers and bring them back.

For More Information

National Association of Resale and Thrift Shops, 153 Halsted, Chicago Heights, IL 60411

Story of the Business

When a chance to "leave the establishment," as she puts it, came around, Patricia Owens packed up and left, lock, stock and barrel, for the sticks of Vermont. Although she had previously worked developing educational programs for the Red Cross in Connecticut, she and her husband jumped at the chance to shed their lifestyles and fancy clothes to live in a cabin with no heat or electricity on 40 acres in Vermont.

"It was wonderful," she said of that first year, "I thought, I'm going to do this for the rest of my life." But soon, she got restless doing nothing, and she started to look for a job.

Instead, she found a flea market in nearby West Lebanon, New Hampshire, that rented space to vendors for $14 a week. "I came home, went to my closet and saw this fabulous wardrobe from years of working in the corporate world. I'll sell my clothes," she decided. The clothes were snapped up, and people asked for more. Since she had exhausted her original supply, she started going to thrift shops and yard sales; she could buy any size she wanted. Soon she expanded to five booth spaces and was buying from wholesalers.

"I didn't like not being able to be in the space after 5 P.M., so we started looking for a space of my own," she recalls. They found an old general store in South Strafford, Vermont, about 30 minutes from Hanover, New Hampshire, and Dartmouth College. "It's in the middle of nowhere," Owens admits. They began to renovate and decorate the space. Upstairs there were two apartments to rent out, which helped keep the overhead low.

"A lot of people say my choice to be in this town was pure folly, but I came here because of the vision I had in my head: I wanted to play house," she remarks. "I wanted to have an enchanted Alice in

Wonderland place. and I needed space I could afford."

Indeed, Owens' store looks like a fashionable Victorian grandmother's attic, with clothes that are classic and in style. A selection of vintage clothing for men and women is in the basement. The two dressing rooms once served as meat lockers.

"In the beginning, I picked what I liked, but I learned as I went along," she says. She spends at least one full day on the road looking for clothes for the shop, hitting junior league shops in Connecticut for cashmere sweaters and other consignment shops in Massachusetts and southern New Hampshire.

"Sometimes I buy things that will look wonderful in the store, and not because I think they'll sell," she says. And sometimes they don't. She keeps clothes in the South Strafford shop for six weeks; if they don't sell, she brings them to the West Lebanon flea market, where she has a huge first-floor shop. If they don't sell after a few months, she gets rid of them. "Sometimes clothes get tired and stale, and there's no more room for them. In that case, you have to be ruthless and get rid of them," she indicates. She bags them, donates them to the many thrift shops she buys from and prays she doesn't buy them again.

After she had been in business for awhile, she began to take clothes on consignment. The consignor gets 50 percent of the retail price; both locals and visitors bring in clothes. She pays for consignments once a month if they sell more than $30 and lets it accrue if they sell less. She also offers a running credit. "Consignors are my partners," she says. She had to learn how to say no nicely when a consignor brings in clothes that are not appropriate for the store. She puts consignor money into a separate account; she knows of some shops that have gone out of business because the owners have spent the money owed to consignors.

She personally handles every piece of clothing she accepts, doing whatever's necessary to make the item presentable before she prices it, which includes cleaning, mending and ironing. "I've had people come in and buy back their clothes because they got washed, ironed and depilled. They said it didn't look like the same piece of clothing," reports Owens. "Part of my business is just that: making something awful look good."

Even though the store is distant, the ride is pretty. "People do exactly what I thought they would do," she says. "Women or couples come here for a jaunt. Some come regularly from 90 minutes away." She limits the hours of the store to give her time to travel looking for clothes. "I didn't want to be in a store all the time," she adds.

"You don't have to have something for everybody," she advises. "Go with your own sense of how you like it. Do what's fun for you. I've found that the more I do what seems right to me, the better I do."

Country Business Profile
Pet Toy Manufacturer

Fat Cat Inc.
John & Anne Lika
Colchester, Vermont

Description of Business

A company that manufactures toys for cats.

Ease of Startup

Easy.

Range of Initial Investment

$1,000-$10,000 and up

Time Commitment

Full- or part-time.

Can You Run the Business From Home?

Yes

Success Potential

The field is competitive; you have to do something different in order to stand out.

How to Market the Business

Crafts shows, pet and gift shops, mail order.

The Pros

It's a fun business to be in if you're a cat person.

The Cons

This business can take a long time to build up a following; you shouldn't expect to make much money from it for awhile.

Special Considerations

More and more people are spoiling their cats—and dogs—rotten. This business will allow you to benefit from the craze.

For More Information

Pet Age Magazine, 200 S Michigan Avenue, Suite 840, Chicago IL 60604; 312-663-5676.

Story of the Business

Name three dream country businesses: A general store. An inn. A company that sells cat toys.

Huh? Back up. Cat toys?

John Lika left his job at an Ohio ad agency in 1990 to move to Vermont to take a job as marketing director at Ben & Jerry's Homemade. Though he had always worked for other companies, he and his wife, Anne, a consultant, still harbored a dream of running their own business. Once they moved to Vermont, the dream began to take hold, which may have been inevitable. You see, many Vermonters feel that their state motto should be *Run Your Own Business*; In fact, "Moonlight in Vermont...or Starve!" has been a recent popular bumper sticker, which undoubtedly has contributed to the entrepreneurial explosion in the state. However, an old family holiday tradition that revolved around cat toys doggedly followed them to Vermont, and the Likas turned that tradition into a million dollar business.

Every Christmas, the Likas' friends and family would hold a contest to see who could create the most hysterical cat toy for an extended family of 12 cats; Tammy Faye Bakker—with and without mascara—showed up stuffed with catnip one memorable year. Soon after they moved to Vermont, John and Anne began making cat toys by hand in the evening for their new business called Fat Cat Inc. Their Kitty Hoots toys included endearing characters like Vet the Victim and Toss Perot. "There's a lot of entrepreneurial energy in Vermont, which is something I wasn't aware of before I moved here," says John. The business soon became all-consuming, and he left Ben & Jerry's in 1994 to work full-time for Fat Cat Inc.

The Likas ran the business from home until catnip, boxes,

employees, and meeting space had devoured most of their house except for the bedrooms. They moved to a 3000-square-foot warehouse in May, 1995.

Today, the company has eight employees along with Mel and Chuck, a couple of cats who turn paws up or down on every new toy the Likas design. Something must be working, since Fat Cat Inc. was recently selected as the Official Cat Toy of Sony's new French movie, When The Cat's Away, and their web site www.fatcats.com, receives more than 100,000 visitors each month. Fat Cat, Inc. expanded this fall 1997 by introducing—what else?—dog toys, including Doris the Doggie Doctor, Big Mean Kitty, and Postal Plaything.

John says that there are ups and downs to running a small snow country company that does business around the world. "With technology and transportation, running a business in a remote area is pretty easy," he says. "The downside is that many of our suppliers are hundreds, if not thousands, of miles away. Plus, the cost of living, from groceries to houses, is much higher here than in the Midwest." Most entrepreneurs—urban, rural or in-between—put in countless hours to make their business succeed; John estimates he works around 70 hours a week, seven days a week. Though he likes to ski cross-country, and Anne prefers downhill skiing, they don't have the time to go very often.

Despite the workload, the Likas manage to socialize with friends and neighbors. In fact, their entry into a culture that can sometimes be wary of newcomers was streamlined by the birth of their baby, Katherine, three months after they moved to Vermont. "In a new area, it's easy to find a network that revolves around children," says John.

The advice John has for people who would love to move to snow country and start a business? "Make sure your sales are not dependent upon the region since outside markets are much larger," he says. "And be sure you're well-capitalized."

And having a couple of cats or dogs around for those cold winter nights—or for a bit of entrepreneurial inspiration—can't hurt.

Fat Cat Inc. has been growing steadily since its inception. The company's first-year revenues were $12,000, and the Likas borrowed $10,000 to get the business off the ground in addition to taking out a $20,000 line of credit. Lika would like to evaluate the possibility of presenting a direct stock offering to what he calls "our very large and loyal customer base." His five-year projections for the company include reaching a gross revenue of $5 million or more within five years.